Chicago Cookbook

Taste the Windy City with Easy Chicago Recipes

By
BookSumo Press
All rights reserved

Published by
http://www.booksumo.com

LEGAL NOTES

All Rights Reserved. No Part Of This Book May Be Reproduced Or Transmitted In Any Form Or By Any Means. Photocopying, Posting Online, And / Or Digital Copying Is Strictly Prohibited Unless Written Permission Is Granted By The Book's Publishing Company. Limited Use Of The Book's Text Is Permitted For Use In Reviews Written For The Public.

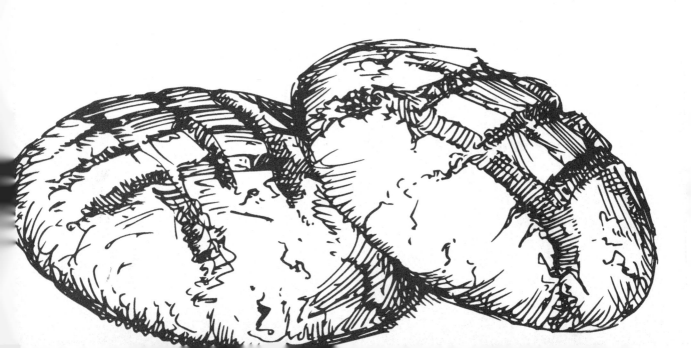

Table of Contents

Plantain Steak Sandwich 7

Hummus Rice Bake 8

Chicken Stroganoff 9

Worcestershire Fondue 10

Crunchy Broccoli Salad 11

Dublin Casserole 12

Broccoli Fries 13

Sloppy Joe's Chicago 14

Tuesday's Casserole 15

Chicago Chicken Cutlets 16

Midway Minestrone 17

Ranch Wontons 18

Pesto Florets Salad 19

Basmati Hearts Rice 20

Windy City Night Stew 21

BBQ Chicken Tots 22

Scaloppini Duck 23

Autumn Mushroom Bake 24

Ginger Ale Stew 25

Picante Slow Cooker 26

Chicago Dump Cake 27

Monday's Ground Beef Macaroni Bake 28

Potato Pot Gratin 29

Carol's Chocolate Cake 30

Smoked Potato and Sausage Gratin 31

Velveeta Casserole 32
4-Ingredient Pot Roast 33
Spicy Garbanzo and Turkey Stew 34
Paseo Tilapia with Salsa 35
Chicken Bop Dip 36
Quick Pot Cake 37
Chicago Roast Dump Dinner 38
Chicago Onion Skillet 39
Golden Chicken Breasts with Shallot Salsa 40
Perfect Pasta Salad 41
Latin Veggies Casserole 42
Rotini Turkey Stew 43
Chicago Breakfast Pitas 44
Teriyaki Wontons 45
Condensed Macaroni Bake 46
Chicken Rice with Cheddar Sauce 47
Chicago Black Bean and Cream Wraps 48
Homemade Blueberry Blintzes 49
Classic Chicken and Broccoli Casserole 50
Bell Beef and Rice Soup 51
Chunky and Cheesy Taco Dip 52
Red Potatoes and Root Vegetables 53
How to Make a Hot Dog Chicago Style 54
Dempster Dip 55
Pizza Skillet 56
Deep Dish Dough 57
Six Corners Pizza 58

Full Macaroni Salad 59
Pizza Skillet 60
Deep Dish Dough 61
Italian Beef Lunch 62
Chicago Restaurant Duck 63
Chicago Cub's Italian Dip 64
Ballpark Salmon 65
Full Italian Beef 66
Maria's Italian Beef 67
Italian Beef II 68
Squash and Steaks in the Pressure Cooker 69
Italian Pizza Minis 70
West Town Spicy Relish 71
Depaul Glazed Meatballs 72
Oatmeal Chocolate Cookies 73
Shrimp Casserole 74
Egg Salad Chicago 75
Chicken with White Glaze 76
Chicago Burgers with Pepper Aioli 77
Illinois Chowder 78
Vanilla Cheesecakes 79
Provolone Chicken Hoagies 80
Alternative Hot Dogs Chicago Style 81
Simple Italian Beef 82
How to Make Beef Au Jus: (Roasted Beef Sauce) 83
Downtown Deli Pizza 84
Illinois Sweet Savory Chili 85

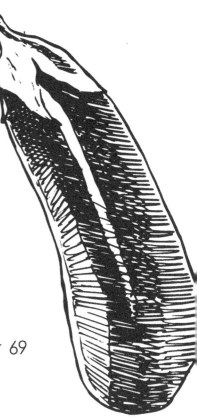

Chicago Chicken Bake 86
Cloud Gate Pizza Sauce 87
Simple Vanilla Cookies 88
Frankfurter Salad Chi-Town Style 89
Alternative Deep Dish 90
Coffee Cakes 101 91
Chicago Tuna Salad 92
Apple Raisins Cookies 93
Garlic Dough for Thin Crusts 94
Homemade Deep Dish 95
Chicago Sirloin 96
Simple Garlic Pizza Crust 97
Italian Style Grilled Chicken 98
Downtown Ribs 99
How to Make Beef Sausages 100
Italian Pepper and Pasta 101

Plantain Steak Sandwich

Prep Time: 10 mins
Total Time: 25 mins

Servings per Recipe: 1
Calories   1219 kcal
Fat   100.4 g
Carbohydrates   65.4g
Protein   23.6 g
Cholesterol   68 mg
Sodium   551 mg

Ingredients

- 2 C. vegetable oil for frying
- 1 green plantain, peeled and halved lengthwise
- 2 tbsp vegetable oil
- 1 clove garlic, minced
- 4 oz beef skirt steak, cut into thin strips
- 1/4 medium yellow onion, thinly sliced
- 1 pinch cumin
- 1 pinch dried oregano
- 1 tbsp mayonnaise
- 1 slice processed American cheese, cut in half
- 2 slices tomato
- 3 leaves lettuce

Directions

1. Place a large pan over medium heat. Heat 2 C. of oil in it. Cook in it the plantains for 2 to 3 min or until they become golden.
2. Drain the plantains and place them on a board. Use a rolling pin or the back of a skillet to flatten them.
3. Place them back in the hot oil and cook them for another 3 min and become golden brown. Drain them and place them aside.
4. Place a large pan over medium heat. Heat in it 2 tbsp of oil. Sauté in it the garlic, skirt steak, onion, cumin and oregano for 8 min while stirring often.
5. Use a knife to spread the mayo over the fried plantains and place one of them on a serving plate.
6. Lay over it the cheese with steak mixture, lettuce, and tomato. Cover them with the second half of the plantain then serve it.
7. Enjoy.

HUMMUS Rice Bake

Prep Time: 10 mins
Total Time: 55 mins

Servings per Recipe: 6
Calories 354.4
Fat 6.3g
Cholesterol 0.0mg
Sodium 438.7mg
Carbohydrates 64.3g
Protein 12.1g

Ingredients

2 (15 - 22 1/2 oz) cans chickpeas, drained and rinsed
3 - 4 C. cooked brown rice
1 (28 oz) cans diced tomatoes, undrained
1 medium white onion, chopped
1 tsp garlic powder
1 tsp dried oregano
1 tsp dried basil
1 - 2 tsp dried parsley
3 tbsp tahini
3 tbsp water
1 tbsp toasted sesame seeds (optional)

Directions

1. Before you do anything, preheat the oven to 375 F. Grease a casserole dish with some olive oil.
2. Get a mixing bowl: Whisk in it the water with the tahini.
3. Combine the remaining ingredients in the casserole dish well. Season them with a pinch of salt and pepper.
4. Spread over it the tahini and water mix. Place it the oven and cook it for 42 min.
5. Top the rice casserole with some sesame seeds then cook them in the oven for an extra 4 min. Serve it warm.
6. Enjoy.

Chicago Stroganoff

Prep Time: 5 mins
Total Time: 8 hr 5 mins

Servings per Recipe: 6
Calories   296.1
Fat   20.6g
Cholesterol   89.8mg
Sodium   879.3mg
Carbohydrates   8.7g
Protein   18.8g

Ingredients

- 1 lb boneless skinless chicken breast, frozen
- 1 (10 1/2 oz) cans cream of mushroom soup, undiluted
- 16 oz sour cream
- 1 (1 oz) package onion soup mix

Directions

1. Grease a slow cooker with some butter. Lay in it the chicken breasts then season them with some salt and pepper.
2. Get a mixing bowl: Whisk in it the soup mix with mushroom soup and sour cream. Pour it over the chicken breasts.
3. Put on the lid and let them cook for 8 h on low. Serve your creamy chicken with some rice.
4. Enjoy.

WORCESTERSHIRE
Fondue

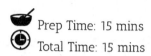

Prep Time: 15 mins
Total Time: 15 mins

Servings per Recipe: 3
Calories   247.3
Fat   18.8g
Cholesterol   59.6mg
Sodium   354.4mg
Carbohydrates   2.4g
Protein   14.3g

Ingredients
4 oz broth
1 tsp chopped garlic
6 oz cheddar cheese
pepper
mustard powder, garnish
Worcestershire sauce, garnish
apple, for dipping

Directions
1. Place a heavy saucepan over medium heat. Stir in it the broth with milk and heat them through.
2. Add the remaining ingredients and mix them well until they cheese melts. Serve your fondue hot.
3. Enjoy.

Crunchy Broccoli Salad

🍲 Prep Time: 10 mins
🕐 Total Time: 20 mins

Servings per Recipe: 6
Calories   240.9
Fat   16.1g
Cholesterol   40.6mg
Sodium   305.0mg
Carbohydrates   21.6g
Protein   6.0g

Ingredients

- 2 bunches broccoli, trimmed
- 1/2 C. balsamic vinegar
- 1/2 C. butter
- 2 tbsp firmly packed brown sugar
- 1/4 tsp salt
- 1/4 tsp ground black pepper

Directions

1. Place the broccoli in a steamer and let it cook for 8 to 10 min.
2. Place a heavy saucepan over medium heat. Stir in it the balsamic vinaigrette and let it cook until half it evaporates.
3. Add the butter, brown sugar, salt and pepper then whisk them until they become smooth.
4. Get a large mixing bowl: Toss in it the broccoli with the dressing then serve it right away.
5. Enjoy.

DUBLIN
Casserole

🥣 Prep Time: 20 mins
🕐 Total Time: 1 hr 10 mins

Servings per Recipe: 8
Calories 343.0
Fat 18.8g
Cholesterol 72.1mg
Sodium 585.9mg
Carbohydrates 26.4g
Protein 16.5g

Ingredients

4 C. chopped cabbage
1 C. sliced celery
1/2 C. chopped onion
1/4 C. butter
8 oz pasta, cooked, drained
1 (12 oz) cans corned beef
4 oz shredded swiss cheese

1/2 C. milk
1/2 tsp dry mustard
1/2 tsp caraway seed
1/4 tsp pepper

Directions

1. Before you do anything, preheat the oven to 350 F.
2. Place a large skillet over medium heat. Melt in it the butter. Cook in it the cabbage, celery and onion for 8 min.
3. Transfer the mix to a greased baking dish. Stir in the rest of the ingredients and mix them well.
4. Cover the pan with a piece of foil and cook it in the oven for 48 min. Serve your corned pasta casserole hot.
5. Enjoy.

Broccoli Fries

Prep Time: 20 mins
Total Time: 40 mins

Servings per Recipe: 6
Calories   0.0
Fat   0.0g
Cholesterol   0.0mg
Sodium   0.0mg
Carbohydrates   0.0g
Protein   0.0g

Ingredients
broccoli
butter
parmesan cheese, to taste

Directions
1. Bring a large salted pot of water to a boil. Cook in it the broccoli for 7 min.
2. Place the a large pan over medium heat.
3. Drain the broccoli from the water. Toss in a large mixing bowl with the parmesan cheese.
4. Cook the broccoli florets in the hot oil for 3 to 5 min. Serve it warm with your favorite dip.
5. Enjoy.

SLOPPY
Joe's Chicago

Prep Time: 20 mins
Total Time: 1 hr 20 mins

Servings per Recipe: 8
Calories   367.2
Fat   77.1mg
Cholesterol   1489.1mg
Sodium   29.9g
Carbohydrates   23.5g
Protein   367.2

Ingredients

- 2 lbs ground beef
- 3 large onions, diced
- 2 large green peppers, diced
- 1/2 C. barbecue sauce
- 2 tbsp Worcestershire sauce
- 1 1/2 tsp mustard
- 1 tbsp sugar
- 3 tbsp vinegar
- 1 1/2 tsp salt
- 20 oz catsup

Directions

1. Place a large pot over medium heat. Cook in it the beef for 10 min over medium high heat.
2. Discard the excess fat. Add to it the remaining ingredients and put on the lid. Let them cook for 1 h 45 min over low heat.
3. Spoon the mix into buns then serve them hot.
4. Enjoy.

Tuesday's Casserole

Prep Time: 15 mins
Total Time: 1 hr 15 mins

Servings per Recipe: 6	
Calories	673.6
Fat	46.8g
Cholesterol	195.0mg
Sodium	891.0mg
Carbohydrates	58.5g
Protein	10.7g

Ingredients

- 1 (14 3/4 oz) cans creamed corn
- 1 (15 1/4 oz) cans whole corn, drained
- 1 C. melted butter
- 3 eggs
- 1 C. sour cream
- 1 tbsp sugar
- 1 (8 1/2 oz) boxes Jiffy corn muffin mix

Directions

1. Before you do anything, preheat the oven to 350 F.
2. Drain the corn and combine it with the remaining ingredients in a greased casserole dish.
3. Place it in the fridge and cook it for 64 min. Serve it hot.
4. Enjoy.

CHICAGO
Chicken Cutlets

Prep Time: 20 mins
Total Time: 1 hr 5 mins

Servings per Recipe: 6
Calories   207.8
Fat   11.1g
Cholesterol   77.3mg
Sodium   76.1mg
Carbohydrates   0.0g
Protein   25.1g

Ingredients
5 -6 chicken breasts
corn flake crumbs
2 eggs
flour

Directions
1. Before you do anything, preheat the oven to 350 F.
2. Place the chicken breasts between 2 pieces of parchment papers. Use a kitchen hammer to flatten them. Season them with some salt and pepper.
3. Beat 2 eggs in a shallow bowl. Spread each of the flour and corn flakes crumbs on a separate shallow bowls.
4. Dust the chicken breasts with flour then dip them in the beaten eggs and coat them with the corn flakes.
5. Place the chicken breasts on a baking pan. Cook them in the oven for 48 min. Serve your chicken breasts warm.
6. Enjoy.

Midway Minestrone

Prep Time: 20 mins
Total Time: 2 hr 20 mins

Servings per Recipe: 8
Calories   301.3
Fat   14.3g
Cholesterol   11.4mg
Sodium   625.5mg
Carbohydrates   35.9g
Protein   10.4g

Ingredients
- 1/4 lb fresh green beans, trimmed and cut into 1 inch pieces
- 2 medium zucchini, trimmed and cut into 1/2 inch dices
- 1 large potato, peeled and cut into 3/4 inch dices
- 1/2 lb cabbage, roughly chopped
- 1/3 C. olive oil
- 3 tbsp butter
- 2 medium onions, chopped
- 3 medium carrots, coarsely chopped
- 3 celery ribs, coarsely chopped
- 2 garlic cloves, minced
- 1 (28 oz) cans Italian plum tomatoes, undrained and chopped
- 3 1/2 C. beef broth
- 1 1/2 C. water
- 1/2 tsp salt
- 1/2 tsp dried basil leaves, crushed
- 1/4 tsp dried rosemary leaves, crushed
- 1/4 tsp fresh black pepper
- 1 bay leaf
- 1 (16 oz) cans cannellini beans
- freshly grated parmesan cheese (optional)

Directions
1. Place a large pot over medium heat. Melt the butter with oil in it. Sauté in it the onion for 7 min.
2. Add the carrots with potato and let them cook for 6 min. Add the celery with beans and let them cook for another 6 min.
3. Add the zucchini and cook them for an extra 4 min. Add the garlic with cabbage then let them cook for 2 min while stirring all the time.
4. Stir in the broth, water and tomato with its juice, basil, rosemary, bay leaf, a pinch of salt and pepper. Cook them until they start boiling.
5. Lower the heat and put on the lid. Cook the stew for 1 h 35 min while stirring from time to time.
6. Once the time is up, drain the canned beans and add it to the pot with the green beans. Cook the stew for an extra 38 min without a lid.
7. Discard the bay leaf then serve your stew hot.
8. Enjoy

RANCH
Wontons

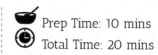 Prep Time: 10 mins
Total Time: 20 mins

Servings per Recipe: 1 batch
Calories   93.2
Fat   6.3g
Cholesterol   13.6mg
Sodium   180.8mg
Carbohydrates   5.1g
Protein   3.7g

Ingredients
1 lb turkey sausage, browned, rinsed and drained.
3/4 C. ranch dressing
1/4 C. mayonnaise
1 C. shredded Monterey jack pepper cheese
1 C. shredded Monterey jack cheese
50 wonton wrappers

Directions
1. Before you do anything, preheat the oven to 350 F.
2. Grease a muffin tin with a cooking spray. Press in it the wonton wrappers to make them in the shape of C..
3. Place the pan in the oven and cook it for 5 min then place them aside.
4. Get a large mixing bowl: Combine in it the remaining ingredients and mix them well. Divide the filling between the wonton C..
5. Place the tin back in the oven and cook them for 4 min then serve them hot.
6. Enjoy.

Pesto Florets Salad

Prep Time: 15 mins
Total Time: 25 mins

Servings per Recipe: 4
Calories	856.8
Fat	14.7g
Cholesterol	91.0mg
Sodium	453.2mg
Carbohydrates	142.3g
Protein	56.5g

Ingredients

- 10 oz basil pesto
- 1 lb penne pasta
- 1 lb broccoli, cut into small florets
- 2 (6 oz) tyson grilled chicken breast strips
- 3 oz shredded parmesan cheese

Directions

1. Slice the broccoli into florets. Place it aside.
2. Cook the pasta according to the directions on the package for 3 min only. Stir in the broccoli florets and cook them for 4 min.
3. Drain the broccoli and pasta from the water. Place the chicken pieces in the pot and cook them for 2 to 3 min to heat them through.
4. Drain the chicken from the water.
5. Get a large mixing bowl: Combine it the broccoli with chicken, pasta, cheese, pesto sauce, a pinch of salt and pepper. Toss them to coat. Serve it right away.
6. Enjoy.

BASMATI
Hearts Rice

Prep Time: 30 mins
Total Time: 1 hr 30 mins

Servings per Recipe: 6
Calories   592.2
Fat   15.0g
Cholesterol   5.6mg
Sodium   1517.9mg
Carbohydrates   98.8g
Protein   18.2g

Ingredients

1/4 C. olive oil
1 medium onions
1 medium red bell peppers
6 garlic cloves, crushed
2 C. brown basmati rice
1 lemons, juiced
3 C. vegetable broth

1 tsp salt
1 tsp black pepper
1 (14 oz) cans artichoke hearts, drained, cut into quarters
2 (15 oz) cans chickpeas, drained
6 tbsp parmesan cheese

Directions

1. Place a large skillet over medium heat. Heat the olive oil in it.
2. Cook in it the rice for 3 min. Stir in the bell pepper with onion for 4 min.
3. Stir in the garlic and cook them for another minute. Add the broth, lemon juice, salt and pepper. Cook them until they start boiling.
4. Put on the lid and cook the rice for 42 min over low heat. Add the artichokes and chickpeas to the pot.
5. Put on the lid and cook them for an extra 6 min. Serve your rice hot with some parmesan cheese.
6. Enjoy.

Windy City Night Stew

Prep Time: 15 mins
Total Time: 4 hr 15 mins

Servings per Recipe: 6
Calories	706.4
Fat	39.1g
Cholesterol	157.3mg
Sodium	1422.3mg
Carbohydrates	39.7g
Protein	43.9g

Ingredients

- 2 lbs beef stew meat, cut in 1 1/2 inch chunks
- 2 medium onions, quartered
- 3 stalks celery, cut in large chunks
- 4 carrots, cut in 1 1/2 inch pieces
- 2 large potatoes, cut in 1 1/2 inch pieces
- 1 C. tomato juice
- 1/4 C. tapioca
- 1 tbsp sugar
- 1 tbsp salt
- 1/4 tsp pepper
- 1/2 tsp dried basil
- 1/2 C. broth
- 1/2 C. water

Directions

1. Before you do anything, preheat the oven to 300 F.
2. Place a large pot over medium heat. Combine all the ingredients except for the potato. Put on the lid and let them cook for 3 h over low heat.
3. Once the time is up, stir in the potato. Cook the stew for an extra 60 min.
4. Serve your stew hot with some rice.
5. Enjoy.

BBQ Chicken Tots

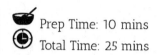

Prep Time: 10 mins
Total Time: 25 mins

Servings per Recipe: 4
Calories   85.6
Fat   2.2g
Cholesterol   86.8mg
Sodium   58.1mg
Carbohydrates   0.4g
Protein   14.9g

Ingredients
1 egg
2 tbsp milk
4 C. barbecue potato chips, crushed
1/2 lb boneless skinless chicken breast, cut into 1 1/2 inch cubes
barbecue sauce

Directions
1. Before you do anything, preheat the oven to 400 F.
2. Mix the milk with egg in a shallow plate.
3. Spread the potato chips in a shallow plate.
4. Coat the chicken breasts with the eggs mix then cover them with the potato chips.
5. Lay the chicken breasts on a cookie sheet. Cook them in the oven for 14 to 16 min then serve them warm.
6. Enjoy.

Scaloppini Duck

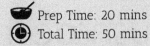

Prep Time: 20 mins
Total Time: 50 mins

Servings per Recipe: 4
Calories   540.2
Fat   5.4g
Cholesterol   138.3mg
Sodium   170.1mg
Carbohydrates   87.2g
Protein   36.6g

Ingredients

- 1 C. buckwheat flour
- 4 tbsp honey
- 4 boneless skinless duck breasts
- 4 C. cooked brown rice
- 1 C. buttermilk

Directions

1. Before you do anything, preheat the oven to 350 F.
2. Flatten the duck breasts with a hammer or pan.
3. Lay 1 tbsp of honey over each breasts. Place them in the buttermilk then drain them and coat them with the buckwheat flour.
4. Lay the duck breasts on a lined up cookie sheet. Cook them in the oven for 35 min. Serve your honey duck breasts warm.
5. Enjoy.

AUTUMN
Mushroom Bake

Prep Time: 15 mins
Total Time: 1 hr 15 mins

Servings per Recipe: 8
Calories 309.9
Fat 12.5g
Cholesterol 30.5mg
Sodium 811.8mg
Carbohydrates 42.3g
Protein 6.8g

Ingredients
2 C. uncooked rice
2 (10 1/2 oz) cans chicken broth
10 1/2 fluid oz water
1/2 C. butter
12 oz canned mushrooms
1 tsp salt
1 medium onion, chopped

Directions
1. Before you do anything, preheat the oven to 350 F.
2. Get a baking pan and grease it with some butter. Combine in it all the ingredients and mix them well.
3. Place the pan in the oven and cook it for 60 min. Serve it hot.
4. Enjoy.

Ginger Ale Stew

Prep Time: 10 mins
Total Time: 6 hr 10 mins

Servings per Recipe: 4
Calories	238.6
Fat	9.8g
Cholesterol	72.5mg
Sodium	628.8mg
Carbohydrates	10.7g
Protein	28.5g

Ingredients
- 1 lb beef stew meat
- 1 can cream of mushroom soup, undiluted
- 1 package onion and mushroom soup mix
- 1/2 C. ginger ale soda
- 3 (4 oz) cans mushroom pieces

Directions
1. Combine the mushroom soup, mushroom/onion soup, mushrooms and ginger ale in a slow cooker.
2. Stir into it the stew meat with a pinch of salt and pepper. Put on the lid and let them cook for 6 h on low.
3. Serve your stew warm with some noodles or rice.
4. Enjoy.

PICANTE
Slow Cooker

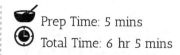
Prep Time: 5 mins
Total Time: 6 hr 5 mins

Servings per Recipe: 6
Calories 124.7
Fat 6.7g
Cholesterol 46.4mg
Sodium 45.6mg
Carbohydrates 0.0g
Protein 15.1g

Ingredients
3 - 4 chicken breasts
1 jar picante sauce

Directions
1. Place the chicken breasts in a greased slow cooker. Pour the sauce all over it.
2. Put on the lid and let it cook for 6 h. Serve your saucy chicken hot.
3. Enjoy.

Chicago Dump Cake

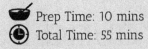

Prep Time: 10 mins
Total Time: 55 mins

Servings per Recipe: 12
Calories 464.8
Fat 23.5g
Cholesterol 30.5mg
Sodium 485.5mg
Carbohydrates 62.6g
Protein 4.1g

Ingredients

- 1 (18 1/4 oz) boxes spice cake mix
- 2 (21 oz) cans apple pie filling
- 1 tsp ground cinnamon
- 1 tsp ground nutmeg
- 1 tsp ground allspice
- 1 tbsp granulated sugar
- 3/4 C. butter
- 1 C. chopped nuts

Directions

1. Before you do anything, preheat the oven to 350 F. Grease a casserole dish with some butter.
2. Get a small mixing bowl: Stir in it the cinnamon, nutmeg, allspice and sugar.
3. Spread the apple pie filling in the casserole dish. Top it with the spice mix followed by the cake mix.
4. Sprinkle the nuts with butter on top. Place the pan in the oven and cook it for 1 h.
5. Serve your pudding cake with some ice cream.
6. Enjoy.

MONDAY'S
Ground Beef Macaroni Bake

Prep Time: 20 mins
Total Time: 1 hr 5 mins

Servings per Recipe: 6
Calories 206.8
Fat 14.1g
Cholesterol 51.4mg
Sodium 355.8mg
Carbohydrates 3.8g
Protein 15.4g

Ingredients
1 box Kraft macaroni and cheese
1 (10 oz) cans cream of mushroom soup
1 lb ground beef
1 (4 oz) cans mushrooms
1/4 chopped onion
salt
pepper
milk, 1 soup can full

Directions
1. Before you do anything, preheat the oven to 350 F.
2. Cook the macaroni according to the directions on the package.
3. In the meantime, place a large skillet over medium heat. Cook in it the beef with onion for 8 min.
4. Get a baking pan and coat it with some butter. Combine in it the cooked beef with mushrooms, cream of mushroom soup, and 1 can of milk.
5. Stir into them the cheese with cooked macaroni, a pinch of salt and pepper.
6. Place the pan in the oven and cook it for 40 to 48 min. Serve it hot.
7. Enjoy.

Potato Pot Gratin

Prep Time: 10 mins
Total Time: 8 hr 10 mins

Servings per Recipe: 8
Calories   240.4
Fat   9.9g
Cholesterol   29.6mg
Sodium   603.4mg
Carbohydrates   30.5g
Protein   8.4g

Ingredients

1 (32 oz) packages frozen hash brown potatoes
2 (10 oz) cans cheddar cheese soup, undiluted
1 (13 oz) cans evaporated milk, undiluted
1 (3 oz) cans French fried onion rings, divided
salt and pepper

Directions

1. Grease a slow cooker with some butter. Place 1/4 C. of onion rings aside.
2. Toss in it the potatoes, soup, milk, the remaining onion rings, a pinch of salt and pepper.
3. Put on the lid and let them cook for 8 h on low. Serve your potato gratin with the remaining onion rings then serve it hot.
4. Enjoy.

CAROL'S
Chocolate Cake

Prep Time: 15 mins
Total Time: 3 hr 15 mins

Servings per Recipe: 8
Calories   388.0
Fat   17.1g
Cholesterol   53.0mg
Sodium   577.2mg
Carbohydrates   57.3g
Protein   5.7g

Ingredients
1 (18 oz) boxes chocolate cake mix
1 C. warm water, divided
3 tbsp oil
2 eggs
1/3 C. chopped nuts (optional)
1/4 C. chocolate syrup
3 tbsp sugar

Directions
1. Get a large mixing bowl: Whisk in it the cake mix, 3/4 C. water, oil and eggs. Fold into it the nuts.
2. Pour the batter in a greased slow cooker.
3. Get another mixing bowl: Whisk in it the chocolate syrup, sugar and 1/4 C. warm water. Pour the mix all over the cake batter.
4. Put on the lid and let them cook for 3 h on low. Serve your cake warm with some ice cream.
5. Enjoy.

Smoked Potato and Sausage Gratin

Prep Time: 10 mins
Total Time: 6 hr 10 mins

Servings per Recipe: 6
Calories   535.6
Fat   33.9g
Cholesterol   66.0mg
Sodium   1456.8mg
Carbohydrates   39.3g
Protein   20.5g

Ingredients

- 2 - 3 large potatoes, peeled and cut into bite sized pieces
- 1 (1 lb) package smoked beef sausage, cut into bite sized pieces
- 2 (14 1/2 oz) cans green beans, drained
- 1 small onion, quartered
- 1 garlic clove, minced
- 2 (10 1/2 oz) cans cream of mushroom soup, undiluted
- 1 C. shredded cheddar cheese

Directions

1. Place the potato in the bottom of a greased slow cooker. Top it with the sausage followed by the green beans, onion, garlic, mushroom soup and cheddar cheese.
2. Put on the lid let them cook for 4 h on low. Serve your gratin warm.
3. Enjoy.

VELVEETA Casserole

Prep Time: 15 mins
Total Time: 35 mins

Servings per Recipe: 30
Calories   126.1
Fat   9.9g
Cholesterol   31.0mg
Sodium   371.5mg
Carbohydrates   1.8g
Protein   7.0g

Ingredients
1 lb Italian turkey sausage
1 lb ground beef
1 lb Velveeta cheese
1 package rye bread

Directions
1. Before you do anything, preheat the oven to 350 F.
2. Place a large skillet over medium heat. Cook in it the sausage with beef for 12 min.
3. Stir into it the cheese until it completely melts. Pour the mix in a greased casserole dish. Lay over it the rye bread.
4. Place the casserole in the oven and cook it for 32 min then serve it hot.
5. Enjoy.

4-Ingredient Pot Roast

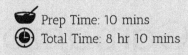

Prep Time: 10 mins
Total Time: 8 hr 10 mins

Servings per Recipe: 6
Calories   21.5
Fat   0.1g
Cholesterol   0.0mg
Sodium   479.1mg
Carbohydrates   5.0g
Protein   1.2g

Ingredients
1 chuck roast
garlic salt (to taste)
pepper (to taste)
1 jar salsa

Directions
1. Sprinkle some garlic salt and pepper all over the roast.
2. Place in it in a greased slow cooker and pour the salsa all over it. Put on the lid and let it cook for 9 h.
3. Once the time is up, drain the roast and shred it then stir it back into the pot or cook it in the oven to make it crispy for about 18 min then serve it hot.
4. Enjoy.

SPICY Garbanzo and Turkey Stew

Prep Time: 15 mins
Total Time: 5 hr 15 mins

Servings per Recipe: 6
Calories   238.3
Fat   1.5g
Cholesterol   70.3mg
Sodium   850.1mg
Carbohydrates   22.0g
Protein   34.3g

Ingredients

1 1/2 lbs turkey tenderloins, cut into 3/4 inch pieces
1 tbsp chili powder
1 tsp ground cumin
3/4 tsp salt
1 (15 oz) cans diced tomatoes with mild green chilies
1 (15 oz) cans garbanzo beans, drained and rinsed (optional)
1 (15 oz) cans black beans, drained but not rinsed
1 (15 1/2 oz) cans pinto beans in chili sauce, un-drained
1 (4 oz) cans mild green chilies (optional)
1 red bell pepper, cut into 3/4 inch pieces
1 green bell pepper, cut into 3/4 inch pieces
3/4 C. onion, chopped
3/4 C. salsa
3 garlic cloves, minced
fresh cilantro (optional)

Directions

1. Combine the turkey tenderloins with chili powder, cumin and salt in a greased slow cooker.
2. Stir into them the beans, tomatoes, chilies, bell peppers, onion, salsa and garlic.
3. Put on the lid and let them cook for 6 h on low.
4. Once the time is up, serve your stew hot.
5. Enjoy.

Paseo Tilapia with Salsa

Prep Time: 15 mins
Total Time: 25 mins

Servings per Recipe: 4
Calories   285.5
Fat   7.6g
Cholesterol   113.5mg
Sodium   1289.5mg
Carbohydrates   9.5g
Protein   47.1g

Ingredients

- 2 lbs tilapia fillets
- 1 1/2 C. tomatoes, chopped
- 1/2 C. green pepper, chopped
- 1/3 C. lemon juice
- 1 tbsp olive oil
- 2 tsp salt
- 2 tsp onions, minced
- 1 tsp basil leaves
- 1/4 C. black pepper, coarsely ground
- 4 drops red pepper sauce
- green pepper ring

Directions

1. Before you do anything, preheat the oven to 500 F.
2. Lay the fish fillets over a lined up cookie sheet.
3. Get a large mixing bowl: Combine in it the tomato with green pepper, lemon juice, olive oil, onion, basil, pepper sauce, a pinch of salt and pepper to make the salsa.
4. Spread the salsa over the fish fillets and cook them in the oven for 7 to 9 min.
5. Serve your baked tilapia fillets with hot with some pepper rings.
6. Enjoy.

CHICKEN
Bop Dip

Prep Time: 20 mins
Total Time: 50 mins

Servings per Recipe: 24
Calories   72.7
Fat   5.8g
Cholesterol   22.5mg
Sodium   57.2mg
Carbohydrates   0.8g
Protein   4.1g

Ingredients
8 oz cream cheese
8 oz sour cream
1 (10 oz) cans white chicken meat, drained
1/2 tsp seasoning salt
1/4 medium onion, minced
1/4 C. parmesan cheese

Directions
1. Before you do anything, preheat the oven to 375 F.
2. Grease a casserole pan with some butter. Combine in it the cream cheese with sour cream, chicken, onion and a pinch of salt.
3. Sprinkle the parmesan cheese on top. Place it in the oven and cook it for 32 min. Serve your dip hot with chips, veggies, bread.
4. Enjoy.

Quick
Pot Cake

Prep Time: 5 mins
Total Time: 3 hr 5 mins

Servings per Recipe: 1
Calories   2221.3
Fat   56.8g
Cholesterol   0.0mg
Sodium   3462.3mg
Carbohydrates   406.7g
Protein   23.4g

Ingredients
1 (18 1/4 oz) boxes cake mix
1 can (12 oz.) soda pop

Directions
1. Grease a slow cooker with a cooking spray.
2. Whisk in it the cake mix with soda until no lumps are found. Put on the lid and cook the cake for 3 h on low.
3. Serve your cake with some ice cream.
4. Enjoy.

CHICAGO
Roast Dump Dinner

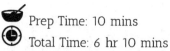

Prep Time: 10 mins
Total Time: 6 hr 10 mins

Servings per Recipe: 6
Calories   800.5
Fat   56.9g
Cholesterol   158.0mg
Sodium   2810.5mg
Carbohydrates   21.4g
Protein   48.7g

Ingredients
3 -5 lbs roast
2 cans cream of mushroom soup
2 cans beef broth
2 packets mushroom soup mix
1 beef bouillon cube
3 cans mushroom pieces, w/juice
1 medium onion, cut into pieces

Directions
1. Whisk the mushroom soup with soup packets and broth in a slow cooker.
2. Add in the roast with bouillon cube, mushroom, onion, a pinch of salt and pepper.
3. Put on the lid and let them cook for 6 h on high. Serve your roast warm.
4. Enjoy.

Chicago Onion Skillet

Prep Time: 7 mins
Total Time: 17 mins

Servings per Recipe: 4
Calories   51.6
Fat   0.4g
Cholesterol   0.0mg
Sodium   54.1mg
Carbohydrates   11.2g
Protein   1.8g

Ingredients

- 1 pint cherry tomatoes, halved
- 1 pint white pearl onion, trimmed
- 1/4 C. chicken broth
- 1/2 tsp superfine ground mustard
- 1/2-1 tsp dried parsley
- 1/4 tsp dried cumin
- salt

Directions

1. Place a large pan over medium heat. Heat in it a splash of broth.
2. Sauté in it the onion for 6 min. Add the tomato then lower the heat and let it cook for 5 while adding more broth if the mix is too dry.
3. Stir in the parsley with mustard, cumin, and a pinch of salt then cook them for another minute.
4. Enjoy.

GOLDEN Chicken Breasts with Shallot Salsa

Prep Time: 10 mins
Total Time: 30 mins

Servings per Recipe: 4
Calories   574.5
Fat   29.4g
Cholesterol   108.8mg
Sodium   1947.9mg
Carbohydrates   37.9g
Protein   38.7g

Ingredients

1 1/2 lbs sweet potatoes, peeled and cut into 2-inch pieces
1 tbsp kosher salt, more to taste
1/2 tsp black pepper, more to taste
4 tbsp olive oil
24 oz chicken breasts, boneless and skinless
4 shallots, sliced into thin rings
2 tbsp rosemary, roughly chopped

Directions

1. Bring a large pot of water to a boil. Cook in it the sweet potato with 1 tsp of salt for 18 min until it becomes tender.
2. Drain the potato and place it aside. Reserve 1/4 C. of the cooking liquid.
3. Place a large pan over medium heat. Melt 1 tbsp of butter in it. Sprinkle some salt and pepper over the chicken breasts.
4. Place them in the hot pan and let them cook for 8 to 9 min on each side. Drain the chicken breasts and place them aside.
5. Heat 3 tbsp of oil in the same skillet. Sauté in it the shallots, rosemary, 1/2 tsp salt, and 1/4 tsp pepper for 4 min to make the salsa.
6. Serve your chicken breasts with the sweet potatoes and shallots salsa.
7. Enjoy.

Perfect Pasta Salad

Prep Time: 30 mins
Total Time: 1 hr

Servings per Recipe: 12
Calories   213.1
Fat   5.7g
Cholesterol   7.7mg
Sodium   107.4mg
Carbohydrates   33.4g
Protein   6.5g

Ingredients

- 6 slices turkey bacon
- 1 1/4 C. Miracle Whip
- 2 tbsp sugar
- 1/2 tsp garlic salt
- 1 (16 oz) packages pasta, cooked and drained
- 3 carrots, shredded
- 1 green pepper, chopped
- 1 onion, chopped

Directions

1. Place a large pan over medium heat. Cook in it the bacon until it become crisp. Drain it and place it aside.
2. Get a large mixing bowl: Combine in it 2 tbsp of the bacon fat with the dressing, sugar and garlic salt.
3. Stir in the miracle whip with pasta, carrot, pepper and onion. Toss them to coat.
4. Place the pasta in the fridge for 32 min. Garnish it with bacon then serve it.
5. Enjoy.

LATIN Veggies Casserole

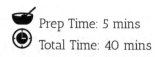
Prep Time: 5 mins
Total Time: 40 mins

Servings per Recipe: 6
Calories   218.0
Fat   1.7g
Cholesterol   0.0mg
Sodium   1000.2mg
Carbohydrates   45.9g
Protein   8.9g

Ingredients

2 (11 1/2 oz) cans corn mixed with chopped peppers, drained
1 (14 1/2 oz) cans tomatoes and green chilies, undrained
1 (15 1/2 oz) cans hominy, drained
1 (15 oz) cans black beans, drained and rinsed
1 (4 oz) cans chopped jalapenos, drained
2 tbsp fresh cilantro, chopped

1/2 tsp salt
1/4 tsp pepper
2/3 C. shredded low-fat Mexican cheese blend

Directions

1. Before you do anything, preheat the oven to 350 F.
2. Get a casserole dish and grease it with some butter. Toss in it all the ingredients except of the cheese.
3. Place the casserole in the oven and let it cook for 26 min then serve it hot.
4. Sprinkle the cheese over the veggies mix. Place the casserole back in the oven and let it cook for an extra 8 min then serve it hot.
5. Enjoy.

Rotini Turkey Stew

Prep Time: 15 mins
Total Time: 35 mins

Servings per Recipe: 4
Calories	607.7
Fat	24.6g
Cholesterol	88.3mg
Sodium	1449.9mg
Carbohydrates	63.0g
Protein	35.5g

Ingredients

- 3 tbsp extra virgin olive oil
- 1 green bell pepper, chopped
- 1 small yellow onion, chopped
- 3 large garlic cloves, minced
- 1 1/2 tsp Mexican seasoning
- 2 tbsp onion flakes
- 3/4 lb ground turkey thigh meat
- 28 oz medium salsa
- 1/2 C. water
- 1 tsp chili powder
- 1 tsp dried oregano
- 1 tsp sugar
- 1/2 tsp pepper
- 8 oz rotini pasta, uncooked
- 1 C. cheddar cheese, shredded

Directions

1. Place a large pot over medium heat. Heat the olive oil in it.
2. Cook in it the bell pepper for 3 min. Stir in the onion with garlic and cook them for 4 min.
3. Stir in the seasoning mix with onion flakes and cook them for an extra 2 min.
4. Mix in the turkey meat then cook them for 6 min.
5. Place a large saucepan over medium heat. Stir in it the salsa with water, chili powder, dried oregano, sugar and pepper. Bring them to a boil.
6. Stir the mix into the pot with the turkey and veggies. Stir in the pasta then cook them until they start boiling.
7. Lower the heat and put on the lid. Cook the stew for 16 to 20 min over low heat. Once the time is up, serve it hot.
8. Enjoy.

CHICAGO
Breakfast Pitas

🥣 Prep Time: 5 mins
🕐 Total Time: 15 mins

Servings per Recipe: 1
Calories 855.2
Fat 59.1g
Cholesterol 611.7mg
Sodium 916.8mg
Carbohydrates 41.1g
Protein 39.9g

Ingredients
3 eggs
1 C. broccoli
2 slices muenster cheese
salt and pepper
2 tbsp olive oil
1 pita bread, with no pocket

Directions
1. Place a large skillet over medium heat. Heat the olive oil in it. Sauté in it the broccoli for 6 min.
2. Stir in the eggs with a pinch of salt and pepper and scramble them in the pan. Cook them until the eggs are done.
3. Lay the cheese slices on top and put on the lid. Turn off the heat and let the cheese melt.
4. Transfer the eggs and broccoli mix to a serving plate.
5. Heat a drizzle of olive oil in the same pan. Cook in it the pitta bread until it become golden on both sides for about 2 to 4 min.
6. Serve it with the broccoli and eggs scramble.
7. Enjoy.

Teriyaki Wontons

 Prep Time: 20 mins
 Total Time: 52 mins

Servings per Recipe: 6
Calories   411.8
Fat   8.4g
Cholesterol   66.0mg
Sodium   2473.5mg
Carbohydrates   60.2g
Protein   22.5g

Ingredients

- 1 - 1 1/2 lb ground turkey
- 8 oz teriyaki sauce
- 4 oz water chestnuts, drained and diced
- 1 piece gingerroot, peeled and minced
- 8 oz hoisin sauce
- 12 oz wonton wrappers

Directions

1. Get a large mixing bowl: Combine in it the turkey with the teriyaki sauce.
2. Add to them the chestnuts with gingerroot, a pinch of salt and pepper. Mix them well to make the filling.
3. Divide the filling on the wonton wrappers and wrap them, using water to seal the edges.
4. Place a large skillet over medium heat. Grease it with a cooking spray or some oil. Cook in it the wrappers for 4 to 5 min on each side.
5. Serve your stuffed wrappers with hoisin sauce.
6. Enjoy.

CONDENSED
Macaroni Bake

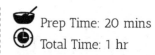
Prep Time: 20 mins
Total Time: 1 hr

Servings per Recipe: 6
Calories 667.2
Fat 34.4g
Cholesterol 96.6mg
Sodium 1533.9mg
Carbohydrates 55.2g
Protein 34.7g

Ingredients

2 C. uncooked elbow macaroni
3 C. cubed cooked chicken
1/2 C. cubed process American cheese
1 small onion, chopped
1/2 C. chopped celery
1/2 C. chopped green bell pepper
1 (8 oz) cans sliced water chestnuts, drained
1 (10 3/4 oz) cans condensed cream of mushroom soup, undiluted
1 (10 3/4 oz) cans condensed cream of chicken soup, undiluted
1 1/3 C. milk
1 (10 1/2 oz) cans chicken broth
1/4 C. butter, melted
2/3 C. crushed saltine
3/4 C. cashew halves

Directions

1. Before you do anything, preheat the oven to 350 F. Grease a casserole dish with some butter.
2. Lay in it the macaroni followed by the chicken on top, American cheese, onion, celery, bell pepper and chestnuts.
3. Get a large mixing bowl: Whisk in it the mushroom soup, chicken soup, milk, a pinch of salt and pepper.
4. Drizzle the mix all over the chestnut layer.
5. Get a mixing bowl: Mix in it the butter with crushed saltine. Sprinkle the mix on top. Place the casserole in the oven and cook it for 38 to 42 min.
6. Serve your macaroni casserole hot with some cashews on top.
7. Enjoy.

Chicken Rice with Cheddar Sauce

Prep Time: 15 mins
Total Time: 8 hr 15 mins

Servings per Recipe: 10
Calories 367.0
Fat 8.6g
Cholesterol 66.8mg
Sodium 1018.3mg
Carbohydrates 42.5g
Protein 28.4g

Ingredients

2 (10 3/4 oz) cans condensed cheddar cheese soup
1 C. water
2 C. salsa

1 1/4 C. uncooked white rice
2 lbs boneless skinless chicken, cubed
10 flour tortillas

Directions

1. Grease a slow cooker with a cooking spray. Stir in it the soup, water, salsa, rice and chicken.
2. Put on the lid and let them cook for 8 h on low.
3. Serve your saucy chicken rice with some tortillas.
4. Enjoy.

CHICAGO
Black Bean and Cream Wraps

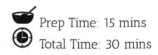

Prep Time: 15 mins
Total Time: 30 mins

Servings per Recipe: 2
Calories   1016.3
Fat   47.6g
Cholesterol   53.2mg
Sodium   1018.6mg
Carbohydrates   114.9g
Protein   36.3g

Ingredients

3 tbsp extra virgin olive oil
2 C. broccoli florets, sliced
1 red bell pepper, sliced
1 green bell pepper, sliced
1 small yellow onion, chopped
2 large garlic cloves, minced
1 tbsp chili powder
1/2 tsp garlic powder

1 (15 oz) cans black beans, rinsed and drained
1/2 C. low-fat sour cream
1/2 C. cheddar cheese, shredded
2 large flour tortillas

Directions

1. Place a large pan over medium heat. Heat the olive oil in it. Sauté in it the bell pepper with broccoli for 4 min.
2. Stir in the garlic with onion and cook them for 5 min. Stir in the chili powder and garlic powder. Cook them for 1 min.
3. Stir in the black beans and heat it through. Turn off the heat. Fold the sour cream with cheddar cheese into the hot mix.
4. Spoon it into tortillas and wrap them then serve them right away with your favorite toppings.
5. Enjoy.

Homemade Blueberry Blintzes

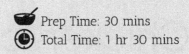

Prep Time: 30 mins
Total Time: 1 hr 30 mins

Servings per Recipe: 1 batch
Calories   4963.0
Fat   231.0g
Cholesterol   1442.3mg
Sodium   5260.5mg
Carbohydrates   542.9g
Protein   179.4g

Ingredients

- 1 lb cream-style cottage cheese
- 1 lb farmer cheese, shredded
- 2 eggs
- 1/4 tsp salt
- 1/4-1/2 C. granulated sugar
- 1/2 tsp vanilla extract
- 1 lemon, juice of
- 1 C. butter, melted and cooled slightly
- 2 eggs
- 1/4 C. milk
- 3 tsp baking powder
- 1/2 C. sugar
- 1 C. flour
- 1 tsp vanilla extract
- sugar
- cinnamon
- 1 (21 oz) cans blueberry pie filling
- 1/2 tsp grated lemon, rind of

Directions

1. Before you do anything, preheat the oven to 300 F.
2. Get a large mixing bowl: Beat in it the cottage cheese with farmer cheese, eggs, sugar, vanilla and salt until they become smooth.
3. Get another mixing bowl: Whisk in it the lemon juice with butter, 2 eggs, milk, baking powder, vanilla, sugar, and flour until no lumps are found.
4. Spread half of the mix in a baking dish. Top it with all of the cheese mix. Spread the remaining flour batter on top.
5. Get a small mixing bowl: Mix in it some sugar with cinnamon. Lay all over the cake pan.
6. Place the baking pan in the oven and cook it for 50 to 60 min.
7. Garnish your cake with the blueberry pie filling and grated lemon after it cools down then serve it.
8. Enjoy.

CLASSIC
Chicken and Broccoli Casserole

 Prep Time: 20 mins
Total Time: 1 hr 5 mins

Servings per Recipe: 4
Calories 591.1
Fat 39.8g
Cholesterol 96.6mg
Sodium 1660.0mg
Carbohydrates 33.0g
Protein 28.4g

Ingredients

2 (10 oz) packages frozen broccoli, steamed
2 C. cooked chicken
2 cans cream of chicken soup
1 C. mayonnaise
1 tsp lemon juice

1/2 C. shredded cheese
1 tbsp butter
breadcrumbs

Directions

1. Before you do anything, preheat the oven to 300 F. Coat a casserole dish with some butter.
2. Place the broccoli in the casserole dish then top it with the chicken.
3. Get a mixing bowl: Whisk in it the mayonnaise with chicken soup, lemon juice, a pinch of salt and pepper. Pour the mix all over the broccoli and chicken mix.
4. Get a mixing bowl: Mix in some breadcrumbs with butter. Spread it all over them then top it with the shredded cheese.
5. Place the casserole in the oven for 48 min. Serve it hot.
6. Enjoy.

Bell Beef and Rice Soup

Prep Time: 15 mins
Total Time: 35 mins

Servings per Recipe: 6
Calories   281.2
Fat   11.7g
Cholesterol   51.4mg
Sodium   390.8mg
Carbohydrates   27.4g
Protein   16.6g

Ingredients

- 1 lb ground beef
- 1/2 chopped onion
- 3 bell peppers, any type
- 14 oz diced tomatoes
- 1 (8 oz) cans tomato sauce
- 1 1/2 C. water
- 1/4 C. balsamic vinegar
- 1/8 tsp salt
- 1/8 tsp black pepper
- 1/4 C. brown sugar
- 1 C. V8 vegetable juice
- 1/2 C. Minute Rice

Directions

1. Place a large skillet over medium heat. Cook in it the beef with onion, garlic, pepper, a pinch of salt and pepper for 12 min.
2. Combine the tomato sauce with water, vinegar, sugar, veggies juice, a pinch of salt and pepper in a large saucepan.
3. Cook them until they start boiling. Stir in the rice and let them cook for 6 min with the lid on.
4. Once the time is up, drain the beef mixture and stir it into the soup pot. Put on the lid and cook it for 16 min over low heat. Serve it hot.
5. Enjoy.

CHUNKY and Cheesy Taco Dip

Prep Time: 15 mins
Total Time: 17 mins

Servings per Recipe: 6
Calories   208.0
Fat   14.4g
Cholesterol   51.3mg
Sodium   549.3mg
Carbohydrates   3.6g
Protein   16.0g

Ingredients

5 oz Swanson white chicken meat packed in water, drained
10 oz mild chunky salsa
1 1/4 oz taco seasoning
2 C. shredded cheddar cheese

Directions

1. Place a heavy saucepan over medium heat. Stir all the ingredients in it and heat everything through for 3 min.
2. Serve your dip with some chips, bread, veggies.
3. Enjoy.

Red Potatoes and Root Vegetables

Prep Time: 10 mins
Total Time: 25 mins

Servings per Recipe: 10
Calories 301.2
Fat 17.4g
Cholesterol 49.3mg
Sodium 654.1mg
Carbohydrates 33.7g
Protein 4.9g

Ingredients

- 8 C. chopped red potatoes
- 4 C. chopped parsnips
- 1 rutabaga, peeled and chopped
- 1 onion, chopped
- 2 tsp salt, divided
- 1 (8 oz) packages cream cheese, softened
- 1/2 C. butter

Directions

1. Bring a large pot of water to a boil with 1 tsp of salt.
2. Stir in it the rutabaga with potato, and parsnips. Put on the lid and let them cook for 14 min over medium heat.
3. Once the time is up, discard the water and transfer the cooked veggies to a large mixing bowl.
4. Add to it the cream cheese with butter and mix them well. Adjust the seasoning of the salad then serve it.
5. Enjoy.

HOW TO MAKE
a Hot Dog Chicago Style

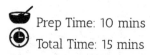

Prep Time: 10 mins
Total Time: 15 mins

Servings per Recipe: 1
Calories	377 kcal
Fat	19.7 g
Carbohydrates	38g
Protein	12.4 g
Cholesterol	30 mg
Sodium	2387 mg

Ingredients

- 1 all-beef hot dog
- 1 poppy seed hot dog bun
- 1 tbsp yellow mustard
- 1 tbsp sweet green pickle relish
- 1 tbsp chopped onion
- 4 tomato wedges
- 1 dill pickle spear
- 2 sport peppers
- 1 dash celery salt

Directions

1. Place a large saucepan of water over medium heat and bring it to a boil. Place a steamer on top and lay the hot dog in it. Let it cook for 3 min.
2. Lay the hot dog in the bun then top it with the yellow mustard, sweet green pickle relish, onion, tomato wedges, pickle spear, sport peppers, and celery salt.
3. Serve your hot dog right away.
4. Enjoy.

Dempster Dip

Prep Time: 15 mins
Total Time: 20 mins

Servings per Recipe: 10
Calories	341 kcal
Fat	24.1 g
Carbohydrates	26.3g
Protein	6.1 g
Cholesterol	18 mg
Sodium	471 mg

Ingredients

- 1 (10 ounce) package frozen chopped spinach, thawed and drained
- 1 C. sour cream
- 1 C. mayonnaise
- 3/4 C. chopped green onions
- 2 tsps dried parsley
- 1 tsp lemon juice
- 1/2 tsp seasoned salt
- 1 (1 lb) loaf round, crusty Italian bread

Directions

1. Get a mixing bowl: Whisk in it the spinach, sour cream, mayonnaise, green onions, parsley, lemon juice, and salt.
2. Place the dip in the fridge until ready to serve. Serve it with some bread or veggies.
3. Enjoy.

PIZZA
Skillet

Prep Time: 30 mins
Total Time: 1 hr 5 mins

Servings per Recipe: 6
Calories   578 kcal
Fat   27.4 g
Carbohydrates   46.8g
Protein   32.3 g
Cholesterol   61 mg
Sodium   1816 mg

Ingredients

1 (1 lb) loaf frozen bread dough, thawed
1 lb Italian turkey sausage, crumbled
2 C. shredded mozzarella cheese
8 ounces sliced fresh mushrooms
1 small onion, chopped
2 tsps olive oil
1 (28 ounce) can diced tomatoes, drained
3/4 tsp dried oregano
1/2 tsp salt

1/4 tsp fennel seed
1/4 tsp garlic powder
1/2 C. freshly grated Parmesan cheese

Directions

1. Before you do anything, preheat the oven to 350 F. Spread the dough in the bottom of a greased oven proof skillet.
2. Place a large pan over medium heat. Cook in it the sausages for 6 min. Drain it and spread it over the dough followed by the mozzarella cheese.
3. Heat the olive oil in the same pan where the sausages were cooked. Sauté in the onion with mushroom for 4 min.
4. Add the tomatoes, oregano, salt, fennel seed and garlic powder. Cook them for 1 min. Spread the mix all over the pizza top it with the parmesan cheese.
5. Cook the pizza skillet in the oven for 30 to 35 min. Serve it hot.
6. Enjoy.

Deep Dish Dough

Prep Time: 10 mins
Total Time: 6 hr 25 mins

Servings per Recipe: 8
Calories	299 kcal
Fat	14.3 g
Carbohydrates	37g
Protein	5.3 g
Cholesterol	0 mg
Sodium	362 mg

Ingredients

- 2 1/4 tsps active dry yeast
- 1 1/2 tsps white sugar
- 1 1/8 C. warm water
- 3 C. all-purpose flour
- 1/2 C. corn oil
- 1 1/2 tsps kosher salt

Directions

1. Get a small mixing bowl: Stir in it the yeast with sugar and warm water let it sit for few minutes to dissolve.
2. Get a large mixing bowl: Mix in it the yeast mixture, flour, corn oil, and kosher salt with your hands or a stand mixer until you get a soft dough.
3. Shape it into a ball and place it in a greased bowl. Lay a kitchen towel over it and let it rise for 6 h.
4. Once the time is up, remove it from the bowl and let it rest for 14 min. Roll the dough into a 10 inch circle then add to it your favorite toppings and cook it!
5. Enjoy.

SIX CORNERS
Pizza

Prep Time: 1 h
Total Time: 1 hr 50 mins

Servings per Recipe: 5
Calories	703 kcal
Fat	30 g
Carbohydrates	75.8g
Protein	30.5 g
Cholesterol	70 mg
Sodium	1646 mg

Ingredients
- 2 tsps white sugar
- 1 C. warm water (110 degrees F/ 45 degrees C)
- 1 tsp active dry yeast
- 3 C. unbleached all-purpose flour, divided
- 1/2 C. warm water (110 degrees F/ 45 degrees C)
- 1/2 C. yellow cornmeal
- 1 1/2 tsps salt
- 2 tbsps olive oil
- 1/4 lb Italian turkey sausage
- 9 ounces shredded mozzarella cheese
- 1/4 C. grated Parmesan cheese
- 1/3 C. diced pepperoni
- 1/4 C. chopped onion
- 1/8 C. chopped green bell pepper
- 1 tsp dried oregano
- 3 cloves garlic, sliced
- 1/2 C. tomato sauce

Directions
1. To prepare the dough: Get a small mixing bowl: Stir in it the sugar with 1 C. f warm water then let it sit to dissolve.
2. Get a large mixing bowl: Mix in it the yeast, 1/2 C. flour, and 1/2 C. warm water. Let them sit for 22 min. Get a mixing bowl: Stir in it the rest of the 2 1/2 C. flour with cornmeal and salt. Reserve half of the mix dry aside.
3. Add the sugar and water mix into the mixture in the bowl and mix them well. Add to it the reserved flour mix and stir them well.
4. Add the flour and yeast mix then combine them well until you get a soft dough. Place the dough on a floured working surface and knead it with your hands for 10 min.
5. Transfer it to an oil greased large bowl and lay a piece of plastic wrap over it. Place it aside until it rises and double. Before you do anything, preheat the oven to 450 F.
6. Get a large mixing bowl: Mix in it the sausage, mozzarella cheese, Parmesan cheese, pepperoni, onion, bell pepper, oregano and garlic to make the filling.
7. Divide the pizza dough into 2 pieces. Press 1 piece of dough into the bottom of a greased baking pan. Place it in the oven and cook it for 5 min. spread over it the filling. Roll the remaining dough pieces and drape it over the filling.
8. Press the edges with a fork. Use a sharp knife to make 2 slits in the top dough piece and pour the tomato sauce all over it.
9. Place the pan in the lower rack and cook it for 46 min. serve your pizza warm.
10. Enjoy.

Full Macaroni Salad

Prep Time: 30 mins
Total Time: 4 hr 40 mins

Servings per Recipe: 10
Calories	197 kcal
Fat	7.4 g
Carbohydrates	26.8g
Protein	6.4 g
Cholesterol	10 mg
Sodium	1143 mg

Ingredients

- 1 (8 ounce) package salad macaroni
- 1 C. small broccoli florets
- 3/4 C. diced Cheddar cheese
- 1/2 C. chopped green bell pepper
- 1/2 C. dill pickle relish, with juice
- 1 large dill pickle, chopped
- 1/2 C. chopped celery
- 1/2 C. sliced black olives
- 1/2 C. sliced green olives (optional)
- 1/4 C. chopped green onion
- 2 tbsps shredded carrot
- 1 tbsp chopped pimento peppers
- 1 C. light mayonnaise
- 1/4 C. prepared yellow mustard
- 1 tsp salt
- 1/2 tsp white sugar
- 1/4 tsp black pepper

Directions

1. Cook the pasta according to the directions on the package. Drain it.
2. Get a large mixing bowl: Toss in it the macaroni, broccoli, Cheddar cheese, green pepper, pickle relish, dill pickle, celery, black olives, green olives, green onion, carrot, and pimento.
3. Get a small mixing bowl: Whisk in it the mayonnaise, mustard, salt, sugar, and black pepper to make the sauce.
4. Add the sauce to the salad and toss them to coat. Place it in the fridge for at least 4 h then serve it.
5. Enjoy.

PIZZA
Skillet

Prep Time: 30 mins
Total Time: 1 hr 5 mins

Servings per Recipe: 6	
Calories	578 kcal
Fat	27.4 g
Carbohydrates	46.8g
Protein	32.3 g
Cholesterol	61 mg
Sodium	1816 mg

Ingredients

- 1 (1 lb) loaf frozen bread dough, thawed
- 1 lb Italian sausage, crumbled
- 2 C. shredded mozzarella cheese
- 8 ounces sliced fresh mushrooms
- 1 small onion, chopped
- 2 tsps olive oil
- 1 (28 ounce) can diced tomatoes, drained
- 3/4 tsp dried oregano
- 1/2 tsp salt
- 1/4 tsp fennel seed
- 1/4 tsp garlic powder
- 1/2 C. freshly grated Parmesan cheese

Directions

1. Before you do anything, preheat the oven to 350 F. Spread the dough in the bottom of a greased oven proof skillet.
2. Place a large pan over medium heat. Cook in it the sausages for 6 min. Drain it and spread it over the dough followed by the mozzarella cheese.
3. Heat the olive oil in the same pan where the sausages were cooked. Sauté in the onion with mushroom for 4 min.
4. Add the tomatoes, oregano, salt, fennel seed and garlic powder. Cook them for 1 min. Spread the mix all over the pizza top it with the parmesan cheese.
5. Cook the pizza skillet in the oven for 30 to 35 min. Serve it hot.
6. Enjoy.

Deep Dish Dough

🥣 Prep Time: 10 mins
🕐 Total Time: 6 hr 25 mins

Servings per Recipe: 8
Calories   299 kcal
Fat   14.3 g
Carbohydrates   37g
Protein   5.3 g
Cholesterol   0 mg
Sodium   362 mg

Ingredients

- 2 1/4 tsps active dry yeast
- 1 1/2 tsps white sugar
- 1 1/8 C. warm water
- 3 C. all-purpose flour
- 1/2 C. corn oil
- 1 1/2 tsps kosher salt

Directions

1. Get a small mixing bowl: Stir in it the yeast with sugar and warm water let it sit for few minutes to dissolve.
2. Get a large mixing bowl: Mix in it the yeast mixture, flour, corn oil, and kosher salt with your hands or a stand mixer until you get a soft dough.
3. Shape it into a ball and place it in a greased bowl. Lay a kitchen towel over it and let it rise for 6 h.
4. Once the time is up, remove it from the bowl and let it rest for 14 min. Roll the dough into a 10 inch circle then add to it your favorite toppings and cook it!
5. Enjoy.

ITALIAN
Beef Lunch

Prep Time: 15 mins
Total Time: 1 hr 25 mins

Servings per Recipe: 4
Calories 417 kcal
Fat 16.1 g
Carbohydrates 36.5g
Protein 30.1 g
Cholesterol 82 mg
Sodium 2119 mg

Ingredients

- 1 1/2 lbs boneless beef chuck, cut into 2-inch pieces
- salt and ground black pepper to taste
- 1 tbsp vegetable oil
- 6 cloves garlic, sliced
- 2 tbsps white vinegar
- 1 tbsp dried oregano
- 1 1/2 tsps salt, or to taste
- 1 tsp dried thyme
- 1 tsp dried rosemary
- 1 tsp freshly ground black pepper
- 1 bay leaf
- 1/4 tsp red pepper flakes, or to taste
- 3 C. chicken broth, or as needed
- 4 ciabatta rolls, sliced in half
- 1 C. chopped giardiniera
- 2 tsps chopped fresh flat-leaf parsley

Directions

1. Sprinkle some sat and pepper all over the chuck roast.
2. Place a large pot over medium heat. Heat the vegetable oil in it and brown in it the meat for 3 to 5 min on each side.
3. Add the garlic, vinegar, oregano, 1 1/2 tsps salt, thyme, rosemary, 1 tsp black pepper, bay leaf, and red pepper flakes.
4. Stir in the broth and put on the lid. Cook them until they start simmering.
5. Put on the lid and cook them for 1 h 25 min over low heat. Pour the mix in a colander to drain the meat. Reserve the broth in the pot.
6. Cut the beef chuck into pieces and cover it with a piece of foil.
7. Place the rolls on a pan. Place on it 1 half of the rolls and spread over them 2 tbsps of the reserved broth for each one.
8. Lay on each roll half a large spoon of the pickled veggies and beef chuck. Cover them with the top buns and place them aside.
9. Heat the beef broth and skim the fat then serve it hot with the sandwiches.
10. Enjoy.

Chicago Restaurant Duck

Prep Time: 15 mins
Total Time: 1 hr 35 mins

Servings per Recipe: 4
Calories 389 kcal
Fat 31.3 g
Carbohydrates 4.5g
Protein 21.8 g
Cholesterol 91 mg
Sodium 163 mg

Ingredients

- 1 (4 lb) whole duck
- 1 tbsp garlic powder
- 1 tbsp onion powder
- salt and pepper, to taste
- 2 tbsps caraway seeds

Directions

1. Before you do anything, preheat the oven to 425 F.
2. Rinse the duck and dry it with some paper towels. Use a sharp knife to score it several times.
3. Sprinkle some garlic powder, onion powder, salt, and pepper inside and outside of the duck. Rub the caraway seeds all over it.
4. Place the duck on a roasting pan with the breast facing down. Let it cook for 16 min. Flip the duck and cook it for an extra 16 min.
5. Lower the oven temperature to 350 F. Cook in it the duck with the breast for an extra 22 min.
6. Flip it to face the breast down and cook it for an extra 22 min. Once the time is up, wrap it in a piece of foil and let it rest for 12 min then serve it.
7. Enjoy.

CHICAGO CUB'S
Italian Dip

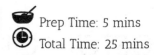
Prep Time: 5 mins
Total Time: 25 mins

Servings per Recipe: 32
Calories   49 kcal
Fat   3 g
Carbohydrates   1.5g
Protein   3.7 g
Cholesterol   16 mg
Sodium   165 mg

Ingredients
1 (1.37 ounce) package McCormick Spaghetti Sauce Mix
1 C. part-skim ricotta cheese
1 egg
2 C. shredded mozzarella cheese, divided
1/2 C. grated Parmesan cheese
1/4 C. mini beef pepperoni slices

Directions
1. Before you do anything, preheat the oven to 375 F.
2. Make the sauce according to the directions on the package.
3. Get a large mixing bowl: Combine in it the ricotta cheese, egg, 1 C. of the mozzarella cheese and Parmesan cheese.
4. Pour the mix in a greased casserole dish. Spread over it 1 C. of mozzarella cheese and pepperoni.
5. Place the pizza casserole in the oven and cook it for 22 min. Serve it with some bread.
6. Enjoy.

Ballpark Salmon

Prep Time: 20 mins
Total Time: 35 mins

Servings per Recipe: 4
Calories	312 kcal
Fat	16.5 g
Carbohydrates	8.8 g
Protein	29.8 g
Cholesterol	83 mg
Sodium	1581 mg

Ingredients
- cooking spray
- 4 (6 ounce) salmon fillets
- 1/4 lemon, juiced
- 2 tsps dried dill weed
- 1/4 C. Dijon mustard
- 2 large dill pickles, diced
- 1/2 white onion, diced
- 1 tomato, seeded and diced
- 4 sport peppers, chopped, or to taste (optional)
- 1 dash celery seed, or to taste

Directions
1. Before you do anything, preheat the oven to 400 F.
2. Get a 4 large pieces of foil and grease them with a cooking spray.
3. Lay the salmon fillets in the foil pieces. Pour over them the lemon juice, dill weed, 1 tbsp mustard, dill pickle, onion, a pinch of salt and pepper.
4. Wrap the foil pieces over the salmon fillets and place them on a cookie sheet. Cook them in oven for 16 min.
5. Once the time is up, place the salmon packets on serving plates. Open them and top them with the diced tomatoes, celery seeds and sport peppers. Serve them hot.
6. Enjoy.

FULL
Italian Beef

🥣 Prep Time: 15 hr 15 mins
⏱ Total Time: 10 hr 45 mins

Servings per Recipe: 7
Calories 657.6
Fat 39.5g
Cholesterol 243.1mg
Sodium 517.7mg
Carbohydrates 3.2g
Protein 67.7g

Ingredients

1 (5 lb) rump roast
1/2 tsp garlic powder
1/2 tsp dried oregano
1/2 tsp coarse-grind black pepper
Sauce
2 C. boiling water
2 beef bouillon cubes
2 tsps dried oregano
1 tsp dried thyme
1/2 tsp coarse-grind black pepper, to taste
1 tsp Tabasco sauce
8 garlic cloves, minced
2 tbsps Worcestershire sauce
salt

Directions

1. Before you do anything, preheat the oven to 325 F.
2. Season the garlic powder, oregano, salt and pepper. Place the roast in a roasting pan and cook it in the oven for 2 h 35 min.
3. Once the time is up, cover the roast with a piece of foil and let it rest for 10 min.
4. Stir the boiling water, bouillon cubes, oregano, thyme, pepper, Tabasco sauce, garlic and Worcestershire sauce into the roasting pan with the remaining drippings from the roast.
5. Place it over medium heat and cook it for 22 min while stirring from time to time to make the gravy.
6. Slice the roast thinly and stir it into the hot gravy. Allow it to cool down for a while then place it in the fridge for at least 8 min.
7. Heat your roast gravy then serve it warm with some steamed or roasted veggies.
8. Enjoy.

Maria's Italian Beef

Prep Time: 10 mins
Total Time: 18 hr 10 mins

Servings per Recipe: 1
Calories	1519.3
Fat	58.9g
Cholesterol	340.2mg
Sodium	2052.1mg
Carbohydrates	119.8g
Protein	121.5g

Ingredients

- 5 lbs rump roast
- 2 (10 1/4 ounce) cans broth
- 1 (1 ounce) package Italian salad dressing mix
- pepperoncini pepper
- 1 jar giardiniera
- 3 -5 sweet green peppers
- 1 loaf long thin French bread

Directions

1. Grease a crockpot with some butter. Stir in it the roast with your broth, Italian dressing mix, pepperoncini, giardiniera, a pinch of salt and pepper.
2. Put on the lid and cook them for 6 h on low. Flip the roast and cook them another 6 h on low.
3. Once the time is up, flip the roast again and let it cook for another 6 h on low.
4. Slice the sweet peppers into 1/8 inch slices and blanch them in some hot water until they become tender. Drain them and place them aside.
5. Slice the bread into 6 inches slices and pull them open. Drain the roast and shred it then spoon it into the bread pieces.
6. Drizzle over it some of sauce from the pot if you desire then serve them hot.
7. Enjoy.

ITALIAN
Beef II

🍲 Prep Time: 30 mins
🕒 Total Time: 6 hr 30 mins

Servings per Recipe: 10
Calories   451.6
Fat   27.5g
Cholesterol   170.1mg
Sodium   354.6mg
Carbohydrates   0.6g
Protein   47.0g

Ingredients

1 tsp salt
1 tsp black pepper, ground
1 tsp oregano
1 tsp basil
1 tsp onion salt
2 - 3 C. water, or broth
1 tsp parsley
1 tsp garlic powder
1 bay leaf
1 (2/3 ounce) package dried Italian salad dressing mix

5 lbs rump roast
3 beef bouillon cubes (optional)
1 green pepper, sliced (optional)

Directions

1. Place a large pot over medium heat. Stir in it the salt, pepper, oregano, basil, onion salt, water, parsley, garlic powder, water, bay leaf and salad dressing mix.
2. Cook them until they start boiling to make the sauce.
3. Grease a slow cooker with a cooking spray. Lay in it the roast and coat it with the sauce. Put on the lid and let it cook for 11 h on low.
4. Once the time is up, discard the bay leaf. Drain the roast and shred it then stir it back into the pot. Stir in the bouillon cubes with pepper.
5. Let it sit for 45 min. Spoon the creamy beef into bread rolls and serve them warm.
6. Enjoy.

Squash and Steaks in the Pressure Cooker

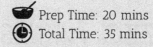

Prep Time: 20 mins
Total Time: 35 mins

Servings per Recipe: 8	
Calories	494.8
Fat	26.4g
Cholesterol	126.7mg
Sodium	874.4mg
Carbohydrates	28.6g
Protein	34.3g

Ingredients

- 2 1/2 lbs round steaks, cut 1/2-inch thick
- 1 C. flour
- 1 tsp salt
- 1/2 tsp pepper
- 1 C. fresh breadcrumb
- 1 1/4 C. chopped onions
- 2 C. finely chopped butternut squash
- 1/4 C. chopped green pepper
- 1/4 C. chopped celery
- 1 tsp salt
- 1 egg, beaten
- 2 tbsps margarine, melted
- 1/4 C. margarine
- 1 C. water

Directions

1. Slice the steaks into 8 pieces in total.
2. Get a shallow dish: Mix in it the flour with 1 tsp salt, and pepper. Dust the steak pieces with the flour mix.
3. Get a large mixing bowl: Mix in it the bread crumbs, onion, squash, green pepper, celery, 1 tsp salt, egg, and 2 tbsps melted margarine. to make the filling.
4. Lay 1/8 of the filling over 1 steak piece and roll it around it tightly. Secure it with a toothpick. Repeat the process with the remaining ingredients.
5. Press the sauté button on a pressure cooker and melt in it 1/4 C. margarine. Lay in it the steak rolls and cook them for 3 to 4 min on each side.
6. Drain them and place them aside. Pour 1 C. of water in the pot and lower in it a steamer basket.
7. Place the browned steak rolls in the basket. Put on the lid and cook them for 16 min. serve them warm with your favorite toppings.
8. Enjoy.

ITALIAN
Pizza Minis

🥣 Prep Time: 15 mins
🕐 Total Time: 30 mins

Servings per Recipe: 4
Calories 417.2
Fat 37.9g
Cholesterol 71.8mg
Sodium 974.1mg
Carbohydrates 3.3g
Protein 16.0g

Ingredients

1 refrigerated thin pizza crust, or homemade
3 1/2 ounces pepperoni
1/2 C. buttermilk ranch dressing
3 green onions, chopped
1/2 C. mozzarella cheese, shredded
1 C. Monterey Jack cheese, shredded

Directions

1. Before you do anything, preheat the oven to 425 F.
2. Lay the dough on a working surface. Pour the ranch dressing all over it. Top it with the pepperoni, green onions and cheese.
3. Roll the dough over the filling and place it on a baking pan. Cook the pizza in the oven for 16 min then serve it warm.
4. Enjoy.

West Town Spicy Relish

Prep Time: 20 mins
Total Time: 20 mins

Servings per Recipe: 1
Calories   359.7
Fat   6.2g
Cholesterol   0.0mg
Sodium   7025.0mg
Carbohydrates   67.5g
Protein   5.1g

Ingredients

- 1/2 peck ripe tomatoes, diced
- 1 C. onion, minced
- 2 green bell peppers, chopped
- 1 hot red pepper, chopped
- 1 1/2 C. celery, chopped
- 1 C. sugar
- 4 tbsps salt
- 3 C. cider vinegar
- 1/2 C. mustard seeds
- 2 tbsps nutmeg
- 2 tsps ground cinnamon
- 1 tsp clove

Directions

1. Drain the tomato from all the juices.
2. Get a mixing bowl: Toss in it the tomato with onions, peppers and celery.
3. Get a small mixing bowl: Whisk in it the sugar and salt, vinegar, mustard seed and spices.
4. Add the mix to the veggies and toss them to coat. Pour it sterilized mason jars and place them in the fridge for a least 3 days before serving it.
5. Enjoy.

DEPAUL
Glazed Meatballs

🥣 Prep Time: 10 mins
🕒 Total Time: 1 hr 40 mins

Servings per Recipe: 6
Calories   535.0
Fat   15.5g
Cholesterol   146.9mg
Sodium   1923.7mg
Carbohydrates   69.0g
Protein   28.8g

Ingredients
Meatball
1 1/2 lbs hamburger
1/4 C. breadcrumbs
2 eggs
1 (1 1/4 ounce) packages onion soup mix
Glazed
1/2 C. brown sugar
1 (12 ounce) jars chili sauce
6 ounces water
1 (16 ounce) cans sauerkraut
1 (16 ounce) cans whole berry cranberry sauce

Directions
1. Before you do anything, preheat the oven to 350 F.
2. Get a large mixing bowl: Combine in it the meatballs ingredients. Shape them into bite size meatballs.
3. Get a mixing bowl: Whisk in it the sauce ingredients.
4. Place the meatballs in a greased casserole dish and pour the sauce all over them. Cook it in the oven for 1 h 35 min. Serve it hot.
5. Enjoy.

Oatmeal Chocolate Cookies

Prep Time: 35 mins
Total Time: 45 mins

Servings per Recipe: 24
Calories   379.9
Fat   21.7g
Cholesterol   28.1mg
Sodium   45.3g
Carbohydrates   3.6g
Protein   379.9

Ingredients

3 1/2 C. flour
3 tsps baking soda
1 tsp salt
1 C. butter
1 C. brown sugar
1 C. sugar
1 egg

1 tbsp milk
2 tsps vanilla
1 C. vegetable oil
1 1/2 C. Rice Krispies
1 1/2 C. oatmeal
12 ounces chocolate chips

Directions

1. Before you do anything, preheat the oven to 350 F.
2. Get a large mixing bowl: Stir in it the flour, baking soda, and salt.
3. Get a mixing bowl: Mix in it the butter, sugars and egg, milk, and vanilla with an electric mixer until they become smooth.
4. Add to it the flour mix with the vegetable oil gradually while alternating between them and mixing at the same time.
5. Fold the cereal, oatmeal and chocolate chips into the mixture. Use a large spoon to place the mixture in the shape of mounds on a lined up baking sheet.
6. Place the cookie in the oven and cook them for 9 to 11 min.
7. Once the time is up, allow the cookies to cool down completely then serve them.
8. Enjoy.

SHRIMP
Casserole

🥣 Prep Time: 1 hr
🕐 Total Time: 1 hr 30 mins

Servings per Recipe: 6
Calories   410.9
Fat   18.9g
Cholesterol   271.0mg
Sodium   16.1g
Carbohydrates   33.5g
Protein   410.9

Ingredients
2 lbs medium shrimp
1/2 C. butter, melted
1/4 C. broth
2 garlic cloves, minced
2 tbsps finely chopped fresh parsley
1 tbsp finely chopped fresh chives
ground nutmeg

salt, to taste
cayenne pepper, to taste
1 C. dry breadcrumbs

Directions
1. Before you do anything, preheat the oven to 350 F.
2. Bring a large pot of water to a boil. Place in it the shrimp and cook it until it starts boiling again.
3. Drain the shrimp, peel it and devein it.
4. Get a large mixing bowl: Whisk in it the butter, broth, garlic, parsley, chives, nutmeg, salt, and cayenne pepper.
5. Combine in the breadcrumbs. Spread half of the cooked shrimp in a greased casserole dish.
6. Spread over it the breadcrumbs mix. Top it with the remaining shrimp and the breadcrumbs mix on top.
7. Place the casserole in the oven and cook it for 32 min. Serve your shrimp casserole hot.
8. Enjoy.

Egg Salad Chicago

Prep Time: 15 mins
Total Time: 20 mins

Servings per Recipe: 3
Calories   307.2
Fat   23.0g
Cholesterol   433.1mg
Sodium   11.9g
Carbohydrates   13.2g
Protein   307.2

Ingredients

6 large eggs, hard-boiled, diced
1/4 C. diced red pepper
1/4 C. diced green pepper
1/2 C. mayonnaise
1 tbsp fresh lemon juice
2 tsps fresh snipped chives
2 tsps chopped fresh dill
1 tsp cider vinegar
salt and pepper

Directions

1. Get a large mixing bowl: Place in it the bell peppers with the chopped eggs.
2. Get a small mixing bowl: Whisk in it the mayo, lemon juice, chives, dill and vinegar.
3. Add the mayo sauce to the salad and toss them gently to combine. Adjust the seasoning of the salad then serve it.
4. Enjoy.

CHICKEN
with White Glaze

🍲 Prep Time: 15 mins
🕐 Total Time: 25 mins

Servings per Recipe: 4
Calories   188.3
Fat   15.0g
Cholesterol   91.9mg
Sodium   9.0g
Carbohydrates   4.5g
Protein   188.3

Ingredients
2 C. meat, minced
cayenne pepper, to taste
1 tbsp bell pepper, seeded and minced
1 egg, beaten with
1 tbsp water
breadcrumbs
White Glaze
4 tbsps butter, melted

4 tbsps flour
1/2 tsp salt
1/8 tsp pepper
1 C. milk

Directions
1. Get a mixing bowl: Mix in it the flour, melted butter, a pinch of salt and pepper.
2. Pour the milk gradually into the mix while whisking all the time.
3. Stir in the minced chicken with bell pepper and seasonings. Shape the mix into bite size pieces.
4. Get a shallow dish: Whisk in it the egg with water. Dip the chicken meatballs in the egg and coat them with the breadcrumbs.
5. Place a deep pan over medium heat. Heat in 1/4 inch of oil until it becomes hot.
6. Cook in it the chicken bites until they become golden brown. Serve your chicken bites with your favorite dip.
7. Enjoy.

Chicago Burgers with Pepper Aioli

Prep Time: 10 mins
Total Time: 50 mins

Servings per Recipe: 8
Calories	260.1
Fat	12.0g
Cholesterol	3.6mg
Sodium	32.9g
Carbohydrates	7.1g
Protein	260.1

Ingredients

- 3 stalks celery, diced
- 1 small onion, diced
- 1/4 C. low sodium soy sauce
- 2 tsps onion powder
- 2 tsps garlic powder
- 1/2 tsp ground black pepper
- 3 C. old fashioned oats
- 12 ounces mushrooms, finely chopped
- 1/2 C. whole wheat flour

Spicy Aoli
- 1/2 C. vegan mayonnaise
- 1/4 C. olive oil
- 1 jarred roasted red pepper, drained
- 1 garlic clove, minced

Directions

1. Place a large saucepan over medium heat. Stir in it 4 C. water, celery, onion, soy sauce, onion powder, garlic powder, and pepper. Cook them until they start boiling.
2. Lower the heat and cook them for an extra 6 min. Add the oats, mushrooms and flour. Let them cook for 6 min.
3. Pour the mix into a large mixing bowl. Place it aside to cool down completely.
4. Before you do anything else, preheat the oven to 350 F.
5. Grease a cookie sheet with some butter. Divide the Veggie mix into 8 portions in the shape of patties.
6. Place the patties on the cookie sheet and cook them for 16 min in the oven.
7. Once the time is up, turn over the patties and cook them for 11 min. Allow the patties to lose heat completely.
8. Before you do anything, preheat the grill.
9. Cover the grill grates with a piece of foil and coat it with a cooking spray. Place the burgers over it and cook them for 8 min on each side.
10. Get a food processor: Combine in it the pepper aioli and blend them smooth. Serve your burgers warm with the pepper aioli.
11. Enjoy.

ILLINOIS
Chowder

🥣 Prep Time: 20 mins
🕐 Total Time: 1 hr 20 mins

Servings per Recipe: 6
Calories   463.3
Fat   26.7g
Cholesterol   183.1mg
Sodium   1370.2mg
Carbohydrates   12.6g
Protein   42.0g

Ingredients

2 lbs haddock, chunked
2 C. peeled and diced new potatoes
8 tbsps butter
1/4 C. chopped celery leaves
3 bay leaves
4 whole garlic cloves
2 1/2 tsps salt
1/4 tsp white pepper

1 clove garlic, minced
1 C. beef broth
2 C. boiling fish stock
2 C. half-and-half cream
1 1/2 tsps chopped fresh dill, topping

Directions

1. Before you do anything, preheat the oven to 350 F.
2. Place a large oven proof Dutch oven pot over medium heat. Stir in the butter with potato, fish, garlic, vermouth, a pinch of salt and pepper.
3. Combine the celery leaves, bay leaves, and cloves in a piece of a cheesecloth seal it. Add it to the pot.
4. Put on the lid and place the pot in the oven. Let it cook for 55 min.
5. Once the time is up, drain the herbs bag and discard it. Stir in the boiling stock.
6. Place a heavy saucepan over medium heat. Heat in it the half and half for 1 to 2 min without boiling it.
7. Stir the half and half to the fish stew then serve it hot.
8. Enjoy.

Vanilla Cheesecakes

🥣 Prep Time: 20 mins
🕐 Total Time: 1 hr

Servings per Recipe: 12
Calories   122.6
Fat   9.4g
Cholesterol   43.1mg
Sodium   8.1g
Carbohydrates   1.6g
Protein   122.6

Ingredients

8 ounces cream cheese
1 egg
1 tsp vanilla
1/4 C. sugar
1 C. ground nuts

1/4 C. melted butter
3 tbsps sugar
Garnish
cherry pie filling

Directions

1. Before you do anything, preheat the oven to 375 F.
2. Get a large mixing bowl: Combine in it the cream cheese with the egg, vanilla and 1/4 C. sugar. Beat them until they become smooth.
3. Get a mixing bowl: Combine in it the ground nuts with the melted butter and 3 tbsps of sugar to make the crust mix.
4. Grease 12 small cheesecake molds with some butter and press into them the nuts mix to make the crust.
5. Pour the cream cheese mix over the crust. Place the mols on a cookie sheet and cook it in the oven for 15 min.
6. Once the time is up, place the cheesecakes aside to cool down completely.
7. loosen the molds around the cheesecakes and transfer them to a serving plate after they completely cool down.
8. Serve your cheesecakes with your favorite toppings.
9. Enjoy.

PROVOLONE
Chicken Hoagies

⏲ Prep Time: 20 mins
🕐 Total Time: 30 mins

Servings per Recipe: 4	
Calories	439.8
Fat	28.3g
Cholesterol	73.1mg
Sodium	1074.6mg
Carbohydrates	33.5g
Protein	12.5g

Ingredients

8 chicken tenderloins
6 tbsps butter, softened
4 hoagie rolls, split
1/4 tsp oregano leaves
1/4 tsp fresh parsley, minced
12 slices hard salami
provolone cheese, halved lengthwise

1/2 C. pizza sauce
1/3 C. mushroom, fresh, diced, sautéed
1/4 tbsp black olives, chopped

Directions

1. Before you do anything, preheat the oven to 425 F.
2. Lay the tenderloins on a lined up cookie sheet. Cook it in the oven for 6 min. Flip them and cook them for another 6 min.
3. Smooth the butter over the rolls and top them with the minced parsley and oregano. Lay over them the salami and cheese slices with tenderloins.
4. Drizzle the pizza sauce over them followed by the mushroom slices and olives.
5. Serve your hoagies with some extra toppings of your choice.
6. Enjoy.

Alternative Hot Dogs Chicago Style

Prep Time: 10 mins
Total Time: 15 mins

Servings per Recipe: 6
Calories	181.7
Fat	14.8mg
Cholesterol	404.0mg
Sodium	24.1g
Carbohydrates	12.0g
Protein	181.7

Ingredients

- 6 large leaves from one head romaine lettuce
- 6 turkey hot dogs
- 1/2 C. onion, Chopped fine
- 1/2 C. tomatoes, diced
- 1/2 C. pickle, diced
- 1/4 C. jalapeno, seeded and diced
- 4 tbsps Dijon mustard
- 3 ounces cheddar cheese
- celery seed, topping

Directions

1. Place a large pan over medium heat. Grease it with a cooking spray. Place in it the hot dogs and cook them until they are browned on all sides.
2. Get a small mixing bowl: Toss in it the onion with tomato, pickles, jalapeno, and a pinch of salt.
3. Place a hot dog over a lettuce leave followed by 3/4 tbsp of mustard and 1/6 of the veggies mix. Sprinkle the cheese on top.
4. Repeat the process with the remaining ingredients. Serve your hot dogs right away.
5. Enjoy.

SIMPLE Italian Beef

🍲 Prep Time: 1 hr
⏱ Total Time: 5 hr

Servings per Recipe: 1 roast
Calories   0.0
Fat   0.0g
Cholesterol   0.0mg
Sodium   0.0mg
Carbohydrates   0.0g
Protein   0.0g

Ingredients
10 lbs beef boneless round roast
Worcestershire sauce
garlic powder
dried basil
red pepper flakes
water
au jus sauce, next recipe

Directions
1. Before you do anything, preheat the oven to 250 F.
2. Coat the beef roast with Worcestershire sauce followed by garlic powder and dry basil one at a time.
3. Season it with the red pepper flakes, some salt and pepper. Place it in a roasting pan. Cook it for 3 h 30 min.
4. Drain the roast cover it completely with a piece of foil. Place it in the fridge to rest of at least 8 h.
5. Thinly slice the roast and place it in zip lock bags then freeze them until ready to use.
6. Enjoy.

How to Make
Beef Au Jus
(Roasted Beef Sauce)

Prep Time: 5 mins
Total Time: 15 mins

Servings per Recipe: 4
Calories	53
Fat	1.1g
Carbohydrates	0g
Protein	17mg
Cholesterol	401mg
Sodium	2.3g

Ingredients

- 1/4 C. beef fat drippings from roast beef
- 1 1/2 tbsps all-purpose flour
- 2 C. beef broth
- salt and ground black pepper to taste

Directions

1. Get a frying hot then melt your fat in it. Combine in the flour with the fat and stir it completely. Continue stirring and heating until the mixture becomes thick for 4 mins.
2. Add your broth to the pan then turn up the heat to high and get everything boiling completely.
3. Continue to let the contents boil until it becomes a bit thicker then combine in your pepper and salt as needed.
4. Enjoy.

DOWNTOWN DELI
Pizza

Prep Time: 4 hr
Total Time: 4 hr 10 mins

Servings per Recipe: 4
Calories   628.8
Fat   32.6g
Cholesterol   54.5mg
Sodium   1116.6mg
Carbohydrates   55.2g
Protein   28.5g

Ingredients

2 C. all-purpose flour
1/2 C. warm water
1 tsp active dry yeast
1 tsp salt
1/3 C. corn oil

1 tsp pepper
1 tbsp dry oregano flakes
1 (14 ounce) cans diced tomatoes
12 ounces shredded mozzarella cheese

Directions

1. Get a large mixing bowl: Stir in it 1 tsp salt with the yeast and warm water. let them sit for 6 min.
2. Mix in 1/2 C. of flour. Combine in 3/4 flour and corn oil. Once again, mix in the remaining 3/4 C. flour.
3. Place the dough on a floured surface and knead it for 6 min until it become soft.
4. Place the dough in a greased bowl and lay a kitchen towel over it. Let it rest for 2 h.
5. Once the time is up, knead the dough slightly then place it back in the bowl, cover it and let it rest for another 2 h.
6. Before you do anything else, preheat the oven to 475 F.
7. Transfer the dough to a floured working surface and roll it until it become 14 inches.
8. Get a food processor: Place it in the tomato and purée it. Drizzle it all over the pizza crust. Top it with oregano, a pinch of salt and pepper.
9. Lay over it your favorite toppings and top them with the mozzarella cheese.
10. Cook the pizza in the oven for 14 min. Serve it hot.
11. Enjoy.

Illinois Sweet Savory Chili

🥣 Prep Time: 30 mins
🕐 Total Time: 1 hr

Servings per Recipe: 10
Calories 367.6
Fat 18.0g
Cholesterol 61.6mg
Sodium 549.2mg
Carbohydrates 36.1g
Protein 22.7g

Ingredients

- 2 lbs ground beef
- 1 C. yellow sweet onion
- 1 C. sweet bell pepper
- 2 stalks celery, diced
- 1 carrot, diced
- 2 jalapeno peppers, minced
- 2 (28 ounce) cans crushed tomatoes
- 1 (6 ounce) cans tomato paste
- 4 - 8 garlic cloves, minced
- salt and pepper, to taste
- 2 ounces dark chocolate
- 1/8 C. orange juice
- 1/4 C. lime juice
- 1/4 C. lemon juice
- 1/2 tsp salt
- 1 tsp black pepper
- 1 tsp cayenne pepper
- 1 tsp cumin
- 1 tsp thyme
- 1 tsp basil
- 2 tsps oregano
- 1 tsp Hungarian paprika
- 2 tsps Mexican chili powder
- 2 tsps garlic powder
- 1 tsp onion powder
- 2 tsps dried parsley
- 1 tsp dried cilantro
- 1/2 C. brown sugar
- 1/2 C. unsweetened cocoa powder

Directions

1. Get a mixing bowl: Mix in it all the spices including the cocoa powder and sugar.
2. Place a Dutch oven over medium heat. Cook in it the beef for 8 min. Discard the excess fat. Season it with some salt and pepper.
3. Push the browned meat to one side of the pot. Stir the onions, garlic, and jalapenos along with the remaining veggies on the other side of the pot.
4. Let them cook for 5 min then sprinkle over them a pinch of salt and pepper.
5. Add the tomato paste and mix them well. Stir in the crushed tomato followed by the spice mix. Cook them until they start simmering while stirring all the time.
6. Add the Lemon juice, Lime juice and Orange juice with the chocolate pieces. Cook them until the chocolate melt while stirring all the time.
7. Lower the heat and put on the lid. Cook the stew for 8 min. Serve it hot with some grated cheddar cheese.
8. Enjoy.

CHICAGO
Chicken Bake

🥣 Prep Time: 45 mins
⏱ Total Time: 1 hr 45 mins

Servings per Recipe: 8
Calories   251.7
Fat   15.4g
Cholesterol   69.8mg
Sodium   737.5mg
Carbohydrates   6.6g
Protein   20.9g

Ingredients

4 boneless chicken breasts
1 package chopped broccoli, cooked
1 can corn
1 can cream of mushroom soup
1/4 C. milk
1/2 lb Velveeta cheese, diced
1/2 jar mushroom
1 jar pimiento
Ritz crackers, crushed
butter

Directions

1. Bring a large pot of water to a boil. Cook in it the chicken breasts for 20 to 25 min or until they are done.
2. Drain the chicken breasts and shred them.
3. Before you do anything, preheat the oven to 450 F.
4. Combine the shredded chicken, broccoli and corn in the greased baking dish.
5. Place a heavy saucepan over medium heat. Combine in it the soup with milk, cheese, mushrooms and pimentos. Cook it for 4 min.
6. Pour the mix all over the chicken and broccoli mix. Top it with the ritz crackers.
7. Place the dish in the oven and cook it for 62 min. Serve it hot.
8. Enjoy.

Cloud Gate Pizza Sauce

🥣 Prep Time: 2 mins
🕐 Total Time: 2 mins

Servings per Recipe: 2
Calories	190.0
Fat	1.0g
Cholesterol	0.0mg
Sodium	128.5mg
Carbohydrates	45.0g
Protein	7.9g

Ingredients

- 1 (32 ounce) cans tomato puree
- 1 tsp oregano
- 1 tsp basil
- 1 tsp thyme
- 1 tsp marjoram
- 1 tsp garlic powder
- 1 tsp pepper
- salt
- 1 tsp sugar

Directions

1. Get a large mixing bowl: Combine in it all the ingredients and mix them well. Place them sauce in the fridge for 4 h.
2. Use it for your pizzas, lasagna and other dish whenever you desire.
3. Enjoy.

SIMPLE
Vanilla Cookies

Prep Time: 30 mins
Total Time: 42 mins

Servings per Recipe: 1 batch
Calories 167.5
Fat 10.3g
Cholesterol 27.1mg
Sodium 17.8mg
Carbohydrates 17.6g
Protein 1.3g

Ingredients

2 C. unsalted butter, at room temperature
1 1/2 C. sugar, plus extra for topping the cookies
1/4 tsp salt
3 1/2 C. all-purpose flour
2 tsps vanilla extract

Directions

1. Before you do anything, preheat the oven to 350 F.
2. Get a large mixing bowl: Beat in it the sugar with butter until they become light and smooth.
3. Pour the sugar with salt into the bowl and mix them well.
4. Add the flour gradually while mixing all the time until you get a smooth dough.
5. Shape the dough into bite size pieces. Place them on a cookie sheet and cook them for 13 to 14 min or until they are golden brown.
6. Enjoy.

Frankfurter Salad Chi-Town Style

Prep Time: 10 mins
Total Time: 15 mins

Servings per Recipe: 4
Calories	491.8
Fat	41.1g
Cholesterol	47.7mg
Sodium	2400.1mg
Carbohydrates	19.1g
Protein	13.7g

Ingredients

- 1/4 C. yellow mustard
- 2 tbsps vinegar
- 1 tsp sugar
- 4 tbsps vegetable oil
- 1/2 medium red onion, thinly sliced
- 1 C. shredded cabbage
- 1 romaine lettuce hearts, shredded
- 2 tomatoes, diced
- 3 large garlic dill pickles, chopped
- celery salt
- black pepper
- 8 vienna beef hot dogs, sliced into 1-inch-thick slices on an angle

Directions

1. Get a large mixing bowl: Whisk in it the mustard, vinegar, sugar, and about 3 tbsps of vegetable oil.
2. Combine in the onions, cabbage, romaine, tomatoes, and pickles, celery salt and pepper then mix them well.
3. Place a skillet over medium heat. Heat 1 tbsp of oil in it. Sauté in it the hot dog slices for 1 to 2 min on each side.
4. Add the hot dog slices to the salad then serve it.
5. Enjoy.

ALTERNATIVE
Deep Dish

Prep Time: 2 hr
Total Time: 2 hr 50 mins

Servings per Recipe: 8
Calories 676.6
Fat 36.7g
Cholesterol 79.4mg
Sodium 1377.8mg
Carbohydrates 53.9g
Protein 31.5g

Ingredients

Dough
1 C. warm tap water
1/4 ounce active dry yeast
3 1/2 C. flour
1/2 C. course ground cornmeal
1 tsp salt

Toppings
1 lb mozzarella cheese, sliced thin
1 lb Italian turkey sausage, crumbled

1 (14 1/2 ounce) cans diced tomatoes, drained
2 garlic cloves, peeled and minced
5 fresh basil leaves, chopped fine
4 tbsps grated parmesan cheese

Directions

1. Get a large mixing bowl: Stir in the yeast with warm water.
2. Pour 1 C. of flour, all of the cornmeal, salt, and vegetable oil in the same bowl. Combine them well. Add the remaining 1/2 C. of flour and mix them well.
3. Place the dough in a greased bowl and cover it with a kitchen towel. Place it aside to rise for 1 h.
4. Grease a 15 inches baking pan and press the pizza dough into it. Let it sit for 18 min.
5. Before you do anything, preheat the oven to 500 F.
6. Place a large skillet over medium heat. Cook in it the sausage for 8 min. Discard the excess fat.
7. Score the pizza dough several times with a sharp knife. Spread the half of the mozzarella cheese over it followed by the cooked sausage, garlic and the remaining cheese.
8. Lay the tomato slices on top followed by the parmesan cheese. Cook the pizza in the oven for 16 min.
9. Lower the oven temperature to 400 F. Cook the pizza in it for an extra 30 min or until it is done to you liking. Serve it hot.
10. Enjoy.

Coffee Cakes 101

Prep Time: 10 mins
Total Time: 45 mins

Servings per Recipe: 12
Calories   323.5
Fat   15.2g
Cholesterol   52.5mg
Sodium   247.3mg
Carbohydrates   42.8g
Protein   4.6g

Ingredients

- 1/2 C. margarine
- 1 (8 ounce) packages cream cheese
- 1 1/4 C. sugar
- 2 eggs
- 1 tsp vanilla extract
- 1 3/4 C. flour
- 1 tsp baking powder
- 1/2 tsp baking soda
- 1/4 C. milk

Coating
- 1/4 C. sugar
- 4 tbsps flour
- 4 tsps cinnamon
- 4 tbsps margarine

Directions

1. Before you do anything, preheat the oven to 350 F.
2. Get a large mixing bowl: Beat in it the margarine, cream cheese and sugar until they become light and smooth. Add the eggs with vanilla and beat them again.
3. Get a mixing bowl: Stir in it the flour, baking powder and baking soda. Sift the mix over the cream mix with milk gradually while alternating between them and mixing all the time.
4. Get a small mixing bowl: Mix in it the sugar, remaining flour, cinnamon and margarine until they become crumbly.
5. Pour the batter into a greased baking pan. Sprinkle the sugar mix all over it.
6. Place the cake in the oven and let it cook for 38 min. Allow it to cool down completely then serve it with your favorite toppings.
7. Enjoy.

CHICAGO
Tuna Salad

🥣 Prep Time: 5 mins
🕐 Total Time: 10 mins

Servings per Recipe: 8
Calories   53.0
Fat   0.9g
Cholesterol   11.1mg
Sodium   215.4mg
Carbohydrates   1.3g
Protein   9.2g

Ingredients

1/4 C. tomatoes, cubed
1/4 C. chopped dill pickle
2 tbsps chopped onions
1 tsp pickle
celery salt (optional)
1 celery rib, chopped

1 tbsp mayonnaise
1 tbsp mustard
2 (5 ounce) cans light chunk tuna in water

Directions

1. Get a large mixing bowl: Combine in it all the ingredients and toss them to coat.
2. Place the salad in the fridge until ready to serve.
3. Enjoy.

Apple Raisins Cookies

🥣 Prep Time: 20 mins
🕐 Total Time: 1 hr 20 mins

Servings per Recipe: 24
Calories   269.7
Fat   12.0g
Cholesterol   37.9mg
Sodium   144.3mg
Carbohydrates   38.4g
Protein   3.8g

Ingredients

- 1/2 C. raisins
- 1/2 C. chopped dates
- 1/3 C. apple juice
- 1/3 C. water
- 1 C. butter, softened
- 1 1/2 C. brown sugar
- 2 large eggs
- 1/2 tsp vanilla extract
- 1/2 tsp salt
- 1/4 tsp baking soda
- 2 C. flour
- 1/4 C. maple syrup
- 1/4 C. peanut butter
- 2 C. rolled oats
- 1/2 C. butterscotch chips
- 1/2 C. semi-sweet chocolate chips

Directions

1. Get an airtight container: Combine in it the water with dates, raisins and apple juice. Let them soak for at least 24 hrs more.
2. Get a large mixing bowl: Beat in it the butter with brown sugar until it become light and fluffy.
3. Crack in it the eggs with vanilla and beat them again until they become smooth.
4. Get another mixing bowl: Stir in it the salt, baking soda, and flour. Add them to the eggs mix and mix them well.
5. Pour in the maple syrup with peanut butter and oats. Combine them well. Add the soaked raisins, dates and amaretto mix.
6. Fold them into the dough along with the butterscotch and semi-sweet chocolate chips. Cover the dough with a plastic wrap and place it in the fridge for 1 h.
7. Before you do anything else, preheat the oven to 350 F.
8. Shape the dough medium sized balls and place them on lined up baking sheets with parchment paper.
9. Cook the cookies in the oven for 18 to 22 min. Allow them to cool down completely then serve them.
10. Enjoy.

GARLIC Dough for Thin Crusts

Prep Time: 2 hr
Total Time: 2 hr 10 mins

Servings per Recipe: 10
Calories   434.5
Fat   11.7g
Cholesterol   0.0mg
Sodium   121.9mg
Carbohydrates   68.7g
Protein   9.8g

Ingredients
7 C. flour
1/2 tsp salt
1/2 C. olive oil
2 C. warm water
4 tsps yeast
12 ounces broth
8 -10 garlic cloves, very finely minced
cornmeal, for rolling out

Directions
1. Get a large mixing bowl: Stir in it the yeast with warm water and a pinch of salt.
2. Add to them the oil with broth, garlic or basil and Parmesan cheese then mix them well.
3. Add the flour gradually while mixing all the time until you get a smooth dough.
4. Transfer the dough to a greased bowl and cover it with a kitchen towel. Place it aside to rest until it doubles in size.
5. Before you do anything, preheat the oven to 500 F.
6. Place the dough on a floured surface and roll it until it becomes 1/8 inch thick.
7. Pierce the pizza dough several times with a fork then cook it in the oven for 6 to 8 min or until it become golden.
8. Serve your pizza crust with your favorite toppings.
9. Enjoy.

Homemade Deep Dish

Prep Time: 34 mins
Total Time: 57 mins

Servings per Recipe: 1 pizza
Calories   2179.9
Fat   150.3g
Cholesterol   475.6mg
Sodium   6773.2mg
Carbohydrates   50.9g
Protein   164.0g

Ingredients

Midwestern Filling
1 bunch spinach, washed, stems removed, and lightly wilted
8 ounces shredded mozzarella cheese
2 ounces turkey bacon, slices diced
1 tsp oregano
2 garlic cloves, sliced thinly
2 ounces mushrooms, sliced
2 C. buffalo
2 C. moose, or hamburger
Simpler Filling

8 ounces shredded mozzarella cheese
1/4 C. shredded parmesan cheese
1/4 lb Italian turkey sausage, crumbled
1/3 C. pepperoni, pieces
1/4 C. sliced black olives
1/4 C. sliced green olives
5 ounces frozen chopped spinach
1 tsp oregano
1 tbsp chopped parsley
2 C. buffalo, or ground chuck

Directions

1. Before you do anything, preheat the oven to 450 F.
2. Roll the pizza dough that you are using on a floured surface. Press half of it into the bottom of a 14 inches baking pan.
3. Cook the pizza crust in the oven for 3 to 4 min.
4. Get a large mixing bowl: Combine in it the spinach, cheese, Canadian bacon, oregano, garlic, buffalo meat, moose meat and mushrooms.
5. Pour the mix all over the baked pizza crust. Lay over it the second pizza crust and press the edges to seal it.
6. Place the pizza pan in the oven and cook it for 48 min. Allow the pizza pan to lose heat for 6 min then serve it with your favorite toppings.
7. Enjoy.

CHICAGO
Sirloin

Prep Time: 10 mins
Total Time: 20 mins

Servings per Recipe: 4
Calories   1290.2
Fat   84.2g
Cholesterol   474.4mg
Sodium   426.9mg
Carbohydrates   0.6g
Protein   124.5g

Ingredients

4 sirloin steaks
Marinade
Worcestershire sauce
soy sauce
cooking sherry
vinegar
Flavored Butter

2 tbsps butter, softened
2 tbsps blue cheese, crumbled
2 - 3 green onions, finely chopped

Directions

1. Get a large zip lock bag: Place it in the sirloin steaks with a splash of Worcestershire sauce, soy sauce, cooking sherry and vinegar.
2. Seal the bag and place it aside to sit for 35 min.
3. Before you do anything else, preheat the grill.
4. Drain the steaks and cook them on the grill after greasing it for 5 to 6 min on each side.
5. Get a small mixing bowl: Combine in it the butter, cheese and onion.
6. Serve your grilled steaks warm with the blue cheese butter.
7. Enjoy.

Simple Garlic Pizza Crust

Prep Time: 1 hr 40 mins
Total Time: 2 hr 10 mins

Servings per Recipe: 6
Calories   358.0
Fat   8.7g
Cholesterol   20.3mg
Sodium   395.2mg
Carbohydrates   60.8g
Protein   8.3g

Ingredients

- 1 (1/4 ounce) package active dry yeast
- 1 1/4 C. lukewarm water
- 3 1/4 C. flour, plus more for dusting
- 1 tsp sugar
- 1/2 C. cornmeal
- 1 tsp salt
- 4 tbsps unsalted butter, melted
- 1 garlic clove, ground to a paste
- pizza toppings, your choice

Directions

1. Get a large mixing bowl: Stir in the warm water with yeast and stir them.
2. Pour in 1/4 C. flour with sugar and mix them well. Add the rest of the warm water, 3 C. flour, the cornmeal and salt. Mix them well.
3. Add the butter with garlic and mix them well until you get a smooth dough.
4. Place the dough on a floured surface and knead it for at least 14 min until it become soft.
5. Get a large mixing bowl: Grease it with some olive oil and place the dough ball in it. Cover the dough with a plastic wrap and let it rest for 1 h.
6. Knead the dough again for at least 2 min. Press it into the bottom of a greased baking pan. Let it rest for 22 min.
7. Lay over it your favorite toppings and bake it to your liking.

ITALIAN Style Grilled Chicken

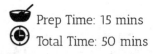

Prep Time: 15 mins
Total Time: 50 mins

Servings per Recipe: 5
Calories   337.0
Fat   21.9g
Cholesterol   44.0mg
Sodium   809.4mg
Carbohydrates   21.7g
Protein   15.9g

Ingredients
5 -6 chicken parts, thighs
1/2 C. mild yellow mustard
1 C. Italian dressing
1/4 C. light brown sugar
2 -3 tbsps Lawry's Seasoned Salt
2 -3 tbsps black pepper
1/4 C. paprika

Directions
1. Before you do anything, preheat the grill and grease it.
2. Get a large mixing bowl: Combine all the ingredients except for the chicken to make the rub.
3. Add the chicken pieces and toss them to coat.
4. Grill the chicken pieces for 10 to 15 min on each side or until they are done to your liking. Serve them warm.
5. Enjoy.

Downtown Ribs

🥣 Prep Time: 30 mins
🕐 Total Time: 3 hr 30 mins

Servings per Recipe: 4
Calories   176.7
Fat   1.4g
Cholesterol   0.0mg
Sodium   847.4mg
Carbohydrates   41.9g
Protein   2.5g

Ingredients

2 full baby back rib racks

Dry Rub
1 tbsp dried mustard
1 tbsp paprika
1 tbsp dark brown sugar
1 1/2 tsps garlic powder
1 1/2 tsps onion powder
1 tsp cayenne pepper
1 1/2 tsps celery salt
1/2 tsp ground allspice
Wood Chips & BBQ Sauce

1 C. hickory chips, soaking in water for 15 min
reserved 2 tbsp dry rub seasonings
1 1/4 C. ketchup
1/4 C. molasses
1/4 C. cider vinegar
1/4 C. water
1/8 tbsp liquid smoke

Directions

1. Remove the membrane on the backside of the ribs.
2. Get a mixing bowl: Mix it the rub mix. Rub the mix into the rubs with your hands.
3. Drain the wood chips and place them in a roasting pan. Put it in the main side of the grill and heat it on high. Place another pan full of water beside it.
4. Let the grill heat for 15 min the turn off the medium flame and high one to medium.
5. Place the ribs on the grill after greasing it. Put on the lid and cook them for 48 min.
6. In the meantime, preheat the oven to 250 F.
7. Fill a roasting pan with water and top it with a wiring rack. Place the rib slabs over it and wrap a large piece of foil around them with the pan.
8. Cook them in the oven for 2 h. Turn off the heat and let them rest for 12 min.
9. Get a small mixing bowl: Whisk in it the spice rub, ketchup, molasses, cider vinegar, water, liquid smoke to make barbecue sauce.
10. Serve the ribs with the sauce.
11. Enjoy.

HOW TO MAKE
Beef Sausages

🥣 Prep Time: 15 mins
🕐 Total Time: 15 mins

Servings per Recipe: 3
Calories   412.7
Fat   32.5g
Cholesterol   109.0mg
Sodium   1250.4mg
Carbohydrates   2.8g
Protein   26.2g

Ingredients
1 1/2 tsps salt
3 1/2 tsps paprika
2/3 tsp garlic powder
2/3 tsp fennel seed
1 tsp ground black pepper
1/4 tsp red pepper flakes
1/2 tsp oregano
1/2 tsp sage
1/2 tsp basil
1/2 tsp thyme
1 lb ground lean beef

Directions
1. Get a large mixing bowl: Place in it the minced beef.
2. Get a small mixing bowl: Combine in it the remaining ingredients well. Add it to the minced beef and mix them well.
3. Wrap the mix in a piece of a plastic wrap and put it in the fridge for an overnight to soak the flavors. Use your sausage as you desire.
4. Enjoy.

Italian Pepper and Pasta

Prep Time: 25 mins
Total Time: 45 mins

Servings per Recipe: 6
Calories   613 kcal
Fat   20.7 g
Carbohydrates   70.8 g
Protein   38.2 g
Cholesterol   92 mg
Sodium   576 mg

Ingredients

- 1 (16 oz.) package rigatoni pasta
- 3 tbsps extra-virgin olive oil
- 1 1/2 lbs skinless, boneless chicken breast, cut in bite-sized pieces
- salt and pepper to taste
- 1 onion, diced
- 3 cloves garlic, minced
- 2 cubanelle pepper, seeded and thinly sliced
- 3 roasted red peppers, drained and chopped
- 2 hot cherry peppers, seeded and minced
- 1 (28 oz.) can crushed tomatoes
- 1/2 C. heavy cream
- 1/2 C. grated Parmesan cheese

Directions

1. Get your pasta boiling in water and salt for 9 mins then remove all the liquids.
2. Top your chicken with some pepper and salt then fry it in olive oil for 8 mins until it is fully done and browned all over.
3. Place the chicken to the side. Then add in the cubanelle pepper, garlic and onions.
4. Cook the mix for 5 mins then add in the crushed tomatoes, cherry pepper, and roast peppers.
5. Get everything simmering then add the cream and the chicken.
6. Let the mix cook for 5 mins then add the pasta and toss everything together.
7. When serving the dish coat it with parmesan cheese.
8. Enjoy.

Made in the USA
Monee, IL
28 October 2021